Samuel Osgood

Book of Vespers

An order of evening worship; with select Psalms and hymns

Samuel Osgood

Book of Vespers
An order of evening worship; with select Psalms and hymns

ISBN/EAN: 9783744785433

Printed in Europe, USA, Canada, Australia, Japan

Cover: Foto ©Lupo / pixelio.de

More available books at **www.hansebooks.com**

BOOK OF VESPERS:

AN ORDER OF EVENING WORSHIP.

WITH

SELECT PSALMS AND HYMNS.

NEW YORK:
JAMES MILLER, 522 BROADWAY.
BOSTON: WALKER, WISE & CO.
1862.

Entered according to Act of Congress, in the year 1862,
By JAMES MILLER,
In the Clerk's Office of the District Court of the United States for the Southern District of New York.

RENNIE, SHEA & LINDSAY,
STEREOTYPERS AND ELECTROTYPERS,
81, 83 & 85 CENTRE-STREET,
NEW YORK.

C. A. ALVORD,
PRINTER.
15 Vandewater-street, New York

PREFACE.

In response to many calls, the Vesper Service as arranged in our volume of "Christian Worship," is here separately published, for the use of such churches as may desire to have it apart from the other liturgical services, which that contains. From the Preface of the original work,* we reprint the following paragraphs, as especially referring to the contents of the present publication, and showing its plan.

"We have here given an extended and careful order of service for Vespers, and have added a full selection from the Psalms for responsive reading, and of Hymns especially adapted to this service. The idea of course is not new, for Vespers are as old as the Christian Church, if not older, and all of the great churches of Christendom, Rome at the head, have their Vesper ritual. Our order is wholly Protestant, and in fact in some respects more bold and progressive than any other of our services; yet it retains much of the severe beauty of the ancient rule, and will be found to wake echoes between the old and new ages. Our esteemed brother, Rev. Samuel Longfellow, formerly of Brooklyn, has been the pioneer in this movement, and we can recognize his labors without sacrificing our own judgment. The Service here given will be found to afford opportunity for the highest art of music, and at the same time to be within the reach of the simplest congregational worship. In fact, the musical portion is so full and varied as to be capable of being sung by any tolerable choir, and may moreover more easily dispense with a choir, and be wholly congregational, than the usual order. The responsive psalms are printed in a new way, so as to be easily used; and this is the first time, within our knowledge, that they have been so arranged as to be read by our people according to the original intention, and it is evident

---

* Christian Worship. Services for the Church: with Order of Vespers, and Hymns.

that this method will soon be universal. These psalms, together with the hymns for congregational singing, contribute towards a more sympathetic and edifying worship in our churches, and tend to do away with the coldness and isolation that are so often complained of. Strange it is that principles so large and genial as ours should be so commonly set forth inadequately, and the most meagre of rituals should attend so rich a faith.

"The Vesper Service may admit of the accustomed evening or afternoon sermon, although it is more compatible with an extemporaneous address or exposition. We believe that it meets a decided and general want in our churches, and attracts and impresses many who do not care to attend an evening service on the old plan, or to hear two regular sermons with much the same accompaniments. The want of something like this has led several churches to discontinue the second service. It is a very serious and devout mode of worship, and only by a monstrous perversion can it be made the occasion of musical vanity and operatic artifice. It is in great part scriptural, and calls for constant and devout attention from the audience. Thus far, wherever held, it has won the favor of all classes of hearers, and is ranked among the fixed institutions of religion with us as with the ancient Church."

We need not say much to illustrate the great breadth and richness of the materials which the Scriptures furnish for this Service, and which are here presented, it seems to us, more fully than in previous manuals, old or new. The associations, for example, that gather around the New Testament Hymns, as here given, are most quickening and edifying. The *Magnificat* brings before us the young Hebrew maiden who was to bear the hope of the world and be the type of all consecrated womanhood. The *Nunc Dimittis* exhibits old age as the memento of the past and the precursor of the future, and the venerable Simeon sings to us the swan song of the old dispensation and the cradle song of the new. The *Gloria in Excelsis* opens to us the angelic world, and summons the hosts of heaven to join in our evening prayer. The Son of God and Son of man himself speaks to us in the *Venite ad me* and the *Beatitudes*, and gives his offer of rest to the weary laborer, and his benediction to all the blessed children of God. The *Te Deum* closes the list, and gives voice to the praise of the whole family of the faithful on earth and in heaven. Surely these images and words well become the peaceful hour of Sabbath evening worship, and unite in themselves and the wealth of music that so many ages have been accumulating about them, a world of comfort, instruction, and inspiration. God grant that such affluence may not be in vain, and our churches may enjoy this precious heritage as never before.

We only add, in conclusion, that if any congregations object at present to the responsive parts of this Service, the objection may be met by the Minister reading the Introduction, and the choir singing a Psalm or Anthem in place of the responsive Psalm.

S. O.
F. A. F.

New York, *March* 21, 1862.

ORDER OF SERVICES.

I. Voluntary on the Organ.
II. Introduction: read by Minister and People standing, and followed by the "Gloria Patri," said or chanted.*
III. Vesper Hymn, from the collection at the end of the book. *Not read. People sit.*
IV. Prayer.
V. Sacred Melody. *Not announced. People sit.*
VI. Selected Psalms. Read by Minister and People *standing*. Ending with the Doxology, "Now unto the King Eternal," &c.*
VII. Reading from Old Testament.
VIII. Chanted Psalm, or corresponding Hymn, as in pages 15 to 21. Other Psalms may be used at discretion. *Not announced. People stand.*
IX. Reading from New Testament.
X. Chanted Hymn from New Testament, or one of the versified Hymns, as in pages 21 to 30: 1. *Magnificat;* 2. *Nunc Dimittis;* 3. *Gloria in Excelsis;* 4. *Venite ad me;* 5. *Beatitudes;* 6. *Te Deum;* or, one of the corresponding versified Hymns. *Not read. People stand.*
XI. Exposition or Address.
XII. Silent Prayer,—closed by
XIII. Chanted Prayer,—usually the Lord's Prayer.
XIV. Congregational Hymn. *Congregation stand and sing.*
XV. Benediction, the AMEN chanted.

* See p. 7 of the Preface.

VESPERS.

The Minister shall read one or more of these Sentences; and then say, with the People responsively, the words of praise that follow: " O Lord, open thou our lips," &c.

FROM the rising of the sun unto the going down of the same, the Lord's name is to be praised.

Let our prayers be set forth in his sight as incense, and the lifting up of our hands, as an evening sacrifice.

Let us therefore come boldly unto the throne of grace, that we may obtain mercy, and find grace to help in time of need.

Behold! God is my salvation; I will trust and not be afraid: for the Lord Jehovah is my strength and my song; he also is become my salvation.

The Lord is nigh unto all them that call upon him, to all that call upon him in truth.

Oh, send out thy light and thy truth: let them lead me; let them bring me unto thy holy hill, and to thy tabernacles.

I am the light of the world: he that followeth me shall not walk in darkness, but shall have the light of life.

Peace be to the brethren, and love with faith from God the Father and the Lord Jesus Christ.

Peace I leave with you, my peace I give unto you; not as the world giveth give I unto you.

God who commanded the light to shine out of darkness, hath shined in our hearts, to give the light of the knowledge of the glory of God in the face of Jesus Christ.

Humble yourselves therefore under the mighty hand of God, that he may exalt you in due time: casting all your care upon him; for he careth for you.

Come unto me, all ye that labor and are heavy laden, and I will give you rest. Take my yoke upon you, and learn of me, for I am meek and lowly of heart; and ye shall find rest unto your souls.

The People standing, the Minister shall say:

O Lord, open thou our lips.
Ans. And our mouth shall show forth thy praise.
Min. O God, haste thee to save us.
Ans. O Lord, make haste to help us.
Min. O Lord, let thy mercy be shown upon us;
Ans. As we do put our trust in thee.
Min. Praise ye the Lord.
Ans. The Lord's name be praised.

Then shall be read, in the order of the month, one of the following Introductions by the Minister and People responsively, each reading a line; or by him alone.

INTRODUCTIONS.

First Sunday.

I WILL lift up mine eyes unto the hills,
From whence cometh my help.
My help cometh from the Lord,
Which made heaven and earth.
He will not suffer thy foot to be moved:
He that keepeth thee will not slumber.

Behold! he that keepeth Israel
Shall neither slumber nor sleep.
The Lord is thy keeper;
The Lord is thy shade upon thy right hand.
The sun shall not smite thee by day,
Nor the moon by night.
The Lord shall preserve thee from all evil:
He shall preserve thy soul.
The Lord shall preserve thy going out, and thy coming in,
From this time forth, and even for evermore.

The Introduction will be followed by the Gloria Patri, thus:

GLORY be to the Father, Almighty God, through Jesus Christ our Lord;
As it was in the beginning, is now, and ever shall be, world without end. *Amen.*

Alleluia! (*The Alleluia to be added especially on joyous occasions.*)

Second Sunday.

LORD, I cry unto thee: make haste unto me;
Give ear unto my voice, when I cry unto thee.
Let my prayer be set forth before thee as incense;
And the lifting up of my hands as the evening sacrifice.
The Lord hath granted his loving-kindness in the daytime;
And in the night-season will I sing of him, and make my prayer unto the God of my life.
Because thy loving-kindness is better than life,
My lips shall praise thee;

My soul shall be satisfied as with marrow and fatness,
　And with joyful lips my mouth shall praise thee;
　When I think of thee upon my bed,
　And meditate upon thee in the night-watches.

(Gloria Patri.)

Third Sunday.

PRAISE ye the Lord! Praise, O ye servants of Jehovah,
　Praise his holy name!
From the rising of the sun to the going down of the same,
　Jehovah's name is to be praised.
　Praise him, all ye his angels;
　Praise him, all ye his hosts!
　Praise ye him, sun and moon;
　Praise him, all ye stars of light!
　Young men and maidens; old men and children
　Let them praise the name of Jehovah!
　For his name alone is exalted;
　His glory is above the earth and heavens.

(Gloria Patri.)

Fourth Sunday.

HOW amiable are thy tabernacles,
　O Lord of hosts!
　My soul longeth, yea even fainteth for the courts of the Lord.
　My heart and my flesh cry out for the living God.

As the sparrow findeth an house,
And the swallow a nest where she may lay her young,
So let me dwell at thine altars,
O Lord of hosts, my King, and my God.
Blessed are the men whose strength is in thee;
In whose heart are thy ways.
They will go from strength to strength,
Till every one of them appeareth in Zion before God.
O Lord of hosts,
Blessed is the man that trusteth in thee.

(*Gloria Patri.*)

Fifth Sunday.

THY word is a lamp unto my feet,
And a light unto my path.
My tongue shall speak of thy word,
For all thy commandments are righteousness
Let thine hand help me;
For I have chosen thy precepts.
I have longed for thy salvation, O Lord'
And thy law is my delight.
Let my soul live, and it shall praise thee;
And let thy judgments help me.
I have gone astray like a lost sheep; seek thy servant!
For I do not forget thy commandments.

(*Gloria Patri.*)

VESPER HYMN,

From the end of the book. Not announced.

PRAYER.

VOLUNTARY BY THE CHOIR.

This should be a Sacred Song, with devout and audible words; and the Air free and expressive.

RESPONSIVE READING OF PSALMS.

The Psalm selected should be distinctly named by the Minister, and read by Minister and People, according to the parallelisms as printed; all STANDING *up. The reading will end with this Doxology:*

Minister. Now unto the King eternal, immortal, invisible, the only wise God;

Answer. Be honor and glory, through Jesus Christ, for ever and ever. *Amen.*

The same Doxology may be used after each Vesper Psalm, unless the Gloria Patri is substituted.

FIRST READING FROM SCRIPTURE.—OLD TESTAMENT.

At the close the Minister will say: "Here endeth this Reading of the Old Testament;" *and the Vesper Psalm will be said or sung in the order of the Month, or the corresponding Hymn. Psalms 110, 111, 112, 113, 114, 115, and 117 have a devotional and musical interest as being the regular Vesper chants for ages. These or any others may be selected.*

VESPER PSALMS.

IN THE ORDER OF THE MONTH.

First Sunday.

Cantate Domino.—Psalm xcviii.

O SING unto the Lord a new song; for he hath done marvellous things.

With his own right hand, and with his holy arm, hath he gotten himself the victory.

The Lord declared his salvation; his righteousness hath he openly showed in the sight of the heathen.

He hath remembered his mercy and truth toward the house of Israel; and all the ends of the world have seen the salvation of our God.

Show yourselves joyful unto the Lord, all ye lands; sing, rejoice, and give thanks.

Praise the Lord upon the harp; sing to the harp with a psalm of thanksgiving.

With trumpets also and shawms, O show yourselves joyful before the Lord, the King.

Let the sea make a noise, and all that therein is; the round world, and they that dwell therein.

Let the floods clap their hands, and let the hills be joyful together before the Lord; for he cometh to judge the earth.

With righteousness shall he judge the world, and the people with equity.

Or this Hymn:

PRAISE. 8s.

LAUDED be thy name forever,
Thou of life the Guard and Giver!
Thou who slumberest not, nor sleepest,
Blest are they thou kindly keepest;
God of stillness and of motion,
Of the rainbow and the ocean,
Of the mountain, rock, and river,
Blessed be thy name forever.

God of evening's yellow ray;
God of yonder dawning day,
That rises from the distant sea,
Like breathings from eternity;
Thine the flaming sphere of light,
Thine the darkness of the night;
God of life, that fade shall never,
Glory to thy name forever!

Second Sunday.

Bonum est confiteri.—Psalm xcii.

IT is a good thing to give thanks unto the Lord, and to sing praises unto thy Name, O Most Highest;

To tell of thy loving-kindness early in the morning, and of thy truth in the night season;

Upon an instrument of ten strings, and upon the lute; upon a loud instrument, and upon the harp.

For thou, Lord, hast made me glad through thy works; and I will rejoice in giving praise for the operations of thy hands.

Or this Hymn:

COME, HOLY SPIRIT. 8s & 7s.

HOLY Spirit, source of gladness,
    Shine amid the clouds of night;
O'er our weariness and sadness
    Breathe thy life and shed thy light!
Send us thine illumination,
    Banish all our fears at length,
Rest upon this congregation,
    Spirit of unfailing strength.

Let that love which knows no measure,
    Now in quickening showers descend,
Bringing us the richest treasure,
    Man can wish or God can send;
Hear our earnest supplication,
    Every struggling heart release,
Rest upon this congregation,
    Spirit of eternal peace!

Third Sunday.

Deus misercatur.—Psalm lxvii.

GOD be merciful unto us, and bless us, and show us the light of his countenance, and be merciful unto us;

That thy way may be known upon earth, thy saving health among all nations.

Let the people praise thee, O God; yea, let all the people praise thee.

O let the nations rejoice and be glad; for thou shalt judge the folk righteously, and govern the nations upon earth.

Let the people praise thee, O God; yea, let all the people praise thee.

Then shall the earth bring forth her increase; and God, even our own God, shall give us his blessing.

God shall bless us; and all the ends of the world shall fear him.

Or this Hymn:

PRAISE. 8s & 7s.

PRAISE to thee, thou great Creator!
　　Praise to thee from every tongue;
Join, my soul, with every creature,
　　Join the universal song.

Father, Source of all compassion,
　　Pure, unbounded grace is thine:
Hail the God of our salvation!
　　Praise him for his love divine.

For ten thousand blessings given,
　　For the hope of future joy,
Sound his praise through earth and heaven,
　　Sound Jehovah's praise on high.

Joyfully on earth adore him,
　　Till in heaven our songs we raise;
There, enraptured, fall before him,
　　Lost in wonder, love, and praise.

Fourth Sunday.

Benedic, anima mea.—Psalm ciii.

PRAISE the Lord, O my soul; and all that is within me, praise his holy Name.

Praise the Lord, O my soul, and forget not all his benefits:

Who forgiveth all thy sin, and healeth all thine infirmities;

Who saveth thy life from destruction, and crowneth thee with mercy and loving-kindness.

O praise the Lord, ye Angels of his, ye that excel in strength; ye that fulfil his commandment, and hearken unto the voice of his word.

O praise the Lord, all ye his hosts; ye servants of his that do his pleasure.

O speak good of the Lord, all ye works of his, in all places of his dominion: praise thou the Lord, O my soul.

Or this Hymn:

PRAYER IN AFFLICTION. 8s & 7s.

LIGHT of those whose dreary dwelling
   Borders on the shades of death,
Come, and by thy love's revealing,
   Dissipate the clouds beneath;
The new heaven and earth's Creator,
   In our deepest darkness rise,
Scattering all the night of nature,
   Pouring eyesight on our eyes.

Still we wait for thine appearing;
   Life and joy thy beams impart,
Chasing all our fears, and cheering
   Every poor, benighted heart:
Come, and manifest the favor
   Promised to thy ransomed race;
Come, thou glorious God and Saviour,
   Come, and bring thy gospel grace.

Fifth Sunday.

Dominus regit me.—Psalm xxiii.

THE Lord is my shepherd; therefore can I lack nothing.

He shall feed me in a green pasture, and lead me forth beside the waters of comfort.

He shall convert my soul, and bring me forth in the paths of righteousness for his Name's sake.

Yea, though I walk through the valley of the shadow of death, I will fear no evil; for thou art with me; thy rod and thy staff comfort me.

Thou shalt prepare a table before me against them that trouble me; thou hast anointed my head with oil, and my cup shall be full.

But thy loving-kindness and mercy shall follow me all the days of my life; and I will dwell in the house of the Lord for ever.

Or this Hymn:

GOD OUR SHEPHERD. 11s.

THE Lord is my Shepherd, no want shall I know:
  I feed in green pastures, safe folded I rest;
He leadeth my soul where the still waters flow;
  Restores me when wandering, redeems when oppressed.

Through the valley and shadow of death though I stray,
  Since thou art my guardian, no evil I fear;
Thy rod shall defend thee, thy staff be my stay,
  No harm can befall with my Comforter near.

In the midst of affliction my table is spread;
  With blessings unmeasured my cup runneth o'er;
With perfume and oil thou anointest my head;
  O what shall I ask of thy providence more?

Let goodness and mercy, my bountiful God,
  Still follow my steps, till I meet thee above;
I seek, by the path which my forefathers trod
  Through the land of their sojourn, thy kingdom
    of love.

SECOND READING.—NEW TESTAMENT.

After this reading, at the close of which the Minister shall say, " Here endeth this Reading of the New Testament," one of the following Hymns from the New Testament shall be sung, or else the Te Deum:

I.
Magnificat.—St. Luke i.

MY soul doth magnify the Lord, and my spirit hath rejoiced in God my Saviour.

For he hath regarded the lowliness of his handmaiden: for, behold! from henceforth all generations shall call me blessed.

For he that is mighty hath magnified me; and Holy is his name.

And his mercy is on them that fear him throughout all generations.

He hath showed strength with his arm; he hath scattered the proud in the imagination of their hearts.

He hath put down the mighty from their seats, and hath exalted the humble and the meek.

He hath filled the hungry with good things; and the rich he hath sent empty away.

Remembering his mercy, he hath holpen his servant Israel,

As he promised to our forefathers, Abraham, and his seed for ever.

Or this Hymn:

MAGNIFICAT. ANCIENT VERSION. C. M.

MY soul and spirit, filled with joy,
   My God and Saviour praise,
Whose goodness did from poor estate
   His humble handmaid raise.

Me blessed of God, the God of power,
   All ages shall confess;
Whose Name is holy, and whose love
   His saints shall ever bless.

The proud and all their vain designs
   He quickly did confound;
He cast the mighty from their seat,
   The meek and humble crowned.

The hungry with good things were filled,
   The rich with hunger pined;
He sent his servant Israel help,
   And called his love to mind;

Which to our fathers heretofore
   His promise did insure,
To Abra'm and his chosen seed
   For ever to endure.

II.

Nunc dimittis.—St. Luke ii.

LORD, now lettest thou thy servant depart in peace, according to thy word:

For mine eyes have seen thy salvation,

Which thou hast prepared before the face of all people;

A light to lighten the Gentiles, and the glory of thy people Israel.

Or this Hymn:

THE BETTER LAND. 7s & 6s.

BRIEF life is here our portion,
   Brief sorrow, short-lived care;
The Life that knows no ending,
   The tearless Life *is there*.
O happy retribution,
   Short toil, eternal rest!
For mortals and for sinners
   A mansion with the Blest!

There God, my King and Portion,
   In fulness of His Grace,
Shall we behold for ever,
   And worship face to face.
Jerusalem the glorious!
   The glory of the elect,
O dear and future vision
   That eager hearts expect.

Jerusalem the only,
   That look'st from Heaven below,

In thee is all my glory,
  In me is all my woe:
O Land that seest no sorrow;
  O State that fear'st no strife!
O princely bowers! O Land of flowers!
  O realm and home of life!

III.

Gloria in excelsis.

GLORY be to God in the highest, on earth, peace, good will toward men.

Or this:

GLORY be to God on high, and on earth peace, good will towards men. We praise thee, we bless thee, we worship thee, we glorify thee, we give thanks to thee for thy great glory, O Lord God, heavenly King, God the Father Almighty. O God, through thy only-begotten Son Jesus Christ, Lamb of God, Son of the Father, that taketh away the sins of the world, have mercy upon us. Through him that taketh away the sins of the world, have mercy upon us. Through him that taketh away the sins of the world, receive our prayer. Through him that sitteth at the right hand of God the Father, have mercy upon us. For thou only art holy; thou only art the Lord; thou only, in Christ, by thy Holy Ghost, art most high in thy glory, O God our Father. Amen.

Or this:

OUR SAVIOUR'S BIRTH.   C. M.

CALM on the listening ear of night
   Come heaven's melodious strains,
Where wild Judea stretches far
   Her silver-mantled plains!

Celestial choirs, from courts above,
   Shed sacred glories there;
And angels, with their sparkling lyres,
   Make music on the air.

The answering hills of Palestine
   Send back the glad reply;
And greet, from all their holy heights,
   The day-spring from on high.

O'er the blue depths of Galilee
   There comes a holier calm,
And Sharon waves, in solemn praise,
   Her silent groves of palm.

"Glory to God!" the sounding skies
   Loud with their anthems sing—
"Peace on the earth—good will to men,
   From heaven's Eternal King."

IV.

Venite ad me.—St. Matt. xi. 28.

COME unto me all ye that labor, and are heavy laden; and I will give you rest.

Take my yoke upon you; and learn of me.

For I am meek and lowly of heart: and ye shall find rest unto your souls.

For my yoke is easy; and my burden light.

Peace I leave with you, my peace I give unto you: not as the world giveth, give I unto you.

Let not your heart be troubled, neither let it be afraid.

Or this Hymn:

INVITATIONS OF JESUS. 7s.

COME, said Jesus' sacred voice,
 Come and make my paths your choice:
I will guide you to your home;
Weary pilgrim, hither come!

Thou, who, houseless, sole, forlorn,
Long hast borne the proud world's scorn,
Long hast roamed the barren waste,
Weary pilgrim, hither haste!

Ye, who, tossed on beds of pain,
Seek for ease, but seek in vain;
Ye, whose swoln and sleepless eyes
Watch to see the morning rise:

Ye, by fiercer anguish torn,
In remorse for guilt who mourn,
Here repose your heavy care:
A wounded spirit who can bear?

Sinner, come! for here is found
Balm that flows for every wound;
Peace that ever shall endure,
Rest eternal, sacred, sure.

V.

Beatitudes.

BLESSED are the poor in spirit: for theirs is the kingdom of heaven.

Blessed are they that mourn: for they shall be comforted.

Blessed are the meek: for they shall inherit the earth.

Blessed are they that do hunger and thirst after righteousness: for they shall be filled.

Blessed are the merciful: for they shall obtain mercy.

Blessed are the pure in heart: for they shall see God.

Blessed are the peace-makers; for they shall be called the children of God.

Blessed are they that are persecuted for righteousness' sake: for theirs is the kingdom of heaven.

Or this Hymn:

COME, YE DISCONSOLATE.   P. M.

COME, ye disconsolate, where'er ye languish;
  Come, at the shrine of God fervently kneel;
Here bring your wounded hearts, here tell your
      anguish;
  Earth has no sorrow that heaven cannot heal.

Joy of the desolate, light of the straying,
  Hope, when all others die, fadeless and pure,
Here speaks the Comforter, in God's name saying,
  Earth has no sorrow that heaven cannot cure.

Here see the bread of life; see waters flowing
  Forth from the throne of God, living and pure;
Come to the feast of love; come, ever knowing,
  Earth has no sorrow that heaven cannot cure.

VI.

Te Deum laudamus.

WE praise thee, O God! we acknowledge thee to be the Lord.

All the earth doth worship thee, the Father everlasting.

To thee all angels cry aloud, the heavens and all the powers therein.

To thee cherubim and seraphim continually do cry,

Holy, holy, holy, Lord God of hosts!

Heaven and earth are full of the majesty of thy glory.

The glorious company of the apostles, praise thee.

The goodly fellowship of the prophets, praise thee.

The noble army of martyrs, praise thee.

The holy church, throughout all the world, doth acknowledge thee,

The Father of an infinite majesty;

Thy holy, true, and only Son;

Also, the Holy Ghost, the Comforter.

Thou art the King of Glory, O God!

And Jesus Christ thy well-beloved Son.

When thou gavest him to deliver man, it pleased thee that he should be born of a virgin.

When he had overcome the sharpness of death, he opened the kingdom of heaven to all believers.

He sitteth at the right hand of God, in the glory of the Father.

We believe that he shall come to be our judge.

We therefore pray thee, help thy servants, whom thou hast redeemed with his precious blood.

Make them to be numbered with thy saints, in glory everlasting.

O Lord, save thy people, and bless thine heritage.

Govern them, and lift them up for ever.

Day by day we magnify thee;

And we worship thy Name, ever, world without end.

Vouchsafe, O Lord, to keep us this day without sin.

O Lord, have mercy upon us; have mercy upon us.

O Lord, let thy mercy be upon us, as our trust is in thee.

O Lord, in thee have we trusted; let us never be confounded.

Or this Hymn:

TE DEUM. C. M.

O GOD, we praise thee, and confess
   That thou the only Lord
And everlasting Father art,
   By all the earth adored.

To thee all angels cry aloud;
   To thee the powers on high,
Both cherubim and seraphim,
   Continually do cry;

O holy, holy, holy Lord,
   Whom heavenly hosts obey,
The world is with the glory filled
   Of thy majestic sway.

The apostles' glorious company,
   And prophets crowned with light,
With all the martyrs' noble host,
   Thy constant praise recite.

The holy church throughout the world,
   O Lord, confesses thee,
That thou eternal Father art
   Of boundless majesty.

THE EXPOSITION OR ADDRESS.

This portion of the Service should refer to the Scriptures that have been read, and is designed to occupy about fifteen minutes. At the close, the Minister will say, " Let us pray;" and the Silent Prayer shall continue a minute or two, after which, without announcement, shall follow the Lord's Prayer, or some other prayer said or chanted.

THE LORD'S PRAYER:

To be said or sung.

OUR Father, who art in heaven,
   Hallowed be thy Name.
Thy kingdom come,
Thy will be done on earth as it is in heaven.
Give us this day our daily bread;
And forgive us our trespasses as we forgive those who trespass against us;
And lead us not into temptation,
But deliver us from evil:
For thine is the kingdom, and the power, and the glory,
For ever and ever. Amen.

CONGREGATIONAL HYMN.

This shall be named by the Minister, with the Air, without being read; and it should be, both in words and music, suited to Congregational singing.

BENEDICTIONS.

THE grace of our Lord Jesus Christ, and the love of God, and the communion of the Holy Spirit, be with us all. *Amen.*

The peace of God, which passeth all understanding, keep your hearts and minds, through Jesus Christ. *Amen.*

Now the God of peace, that brought again from the dead our Lord Jesus, that great Shepherd of the sheep, through the blood of the everlasting covenant, make you perfect in every good work, to do his will, working in you that which is well-pleasing in his sight, through Jesus Christ; to whom be glory for ever and ever. *Amen.*

Grace be with you, mercy and peace from God the Father, and from the Lord Jesus Christ, the Son of the Father, in truth and love. *Amen.*

The grace of our Lord Jesus Christ be with you all. *Amen.*

PSALMS.

The Minister will read the lines beginning at the left, and the People will read the others in response.

At the close of each Reading of the Psalms, shall be repeated the following Doxology:

NOW unto the King eternal, immortal, invisible, the only wise God,
  Be honor and glory, through Jesus Christ, for ever and ever. *Amen.*

PSALM I.

BLESSED is the man
  That walketh not in the counsel of the ungodly,
Nor standeth in the way of sinners,
  Nor sitteth in the seat of the scornful.
But his delight is in the law of the Lord;
  And in his law doth he meditate day and night.
And he shall be like a tree planted by the rivers of water,
  That bringeth forth his fruit in his season;
His leaf also shall not wither;
  And whatsoever he doeth shall prosper.

The ungodly are not so:
> But are like the chaff which the wind driveth away.

Therefore the ungodly shall not stand in the judgment,
> Nor sinners in the congregation of the righteous.

For the Lord knoweth the way of the righteous:
> But the ways of the ungodly shall perish.

PSALM IV.

Hear me when I call, O God of my righteousness:
Thou hast enlarged me when I was in distress;
> Have mercy upon me, and hear my prayer.

O ye sons of men, how long will ye turn my glory into shame?
> How long will ye love vanity, and seek after falsehood?

But know that the Lord hath set apart him that is godly for himself:
> The Lord will hear when I call unto him.

Stand in awe, and sin not:
> Commune with your own heart upon your bed, and be still.

Offer the sacrifices of righteousness,
> And put your trust in the Lord.

There be many that say, Who will show us any good?
> Lord, lift thou up the light of thy countenance upon us.

Thou hast put gladness in my heart,

More than theirs when that their corn and their
    wine increased.
I will both lay me down in peace, and sleep:
    For thou, Lord, only makest me dwell in safety.

PSALM V.

Give ear to my words, O Lord;
    Consider my meditation.
Hearken unto the voice of my cry, my King, and
    my God:
    For unto thee will I pray.
My voice shalt thou hear in the morning, O Lord;
    In the morning will I direct my prayer unto
        thee, and will look up.
For thou art not a God that hath pleasure in wickedness:
    Neither shall evil dwell with thee.
The foolish shall not stand in thy sight:
    Thou hatest all workers of iniquity.
Thou shalt destroy them that speak falsehood:
    The Lord will abhor the bloody and deceitful
        man.
But as for me, I will come into thy house in the
    multitude of thy mercy:
    And in thy fear will I worship toward thy
        holy temple.
Lead me, O Lord, in thy righteousness because of
    mine enemies;
    Make thy way straight before my face.
Let all those that put their trust in thee rejoice:
    Let them ever shout for joy.

Because thou defendest them:
> Let them also that love thy name be joyful in thee.

For thou, Lord, wilt bless the righteous;
> With favor wilt thou compass him as with a shield.

PSALM VIII.

O LORD our Lord, how excellent is thy name in all the earth!
> Who hast set thy glory above the heavens.

Out of the mouth of babes and sucklings hast thou ordained strength,
> That thou mightest still the enemy and the avenger.

When I consider thy heavens, the work of thy fingers,
> The moon and the stars, which thou hast ordained;

What is man, that thou art mindful of him?
> And the son of man, that thou visitest him?

For thou hast made him a little lower than the angels,
> And hast crowned him with glory and honor.

Thou madest him to have dominion over the works of thy hands;
> Thou hast put all things under his feet:

All sheep and oxen,
> Yea, and the beasts of the field;

The fowl of the air, and the fish of the sea;
> And whatsoever passeth through the paths of the seas.

O Lord our Governor.
> How excellent is thy name in all the earth!

PSALM XV.

Lord, who shall abide in thy tabernacle?
    Who shall dwell in thy holy hill?
He that walketh uprightly, and worketh righteousness,
    And speaketh the truth in his heart.
He that backbiteth not with his tongue, nor doeth evil to his neighbor,
    Nor taketh up a reproach against his neighbor.
In whose eyes a vile person is contemned;
But he honoreth them that fear the Lord.
    He that sweareth to his own hurt, and changeth not.
He that putteth not out his money to usury,
Nor taketh reward against the innocent.
    He that doeth these things shall never be moved.

PSALM XVI.

Preserve me, O God:
    For in thee do I put my trust.
O my soul, thou hast said unto the Lord, Thou art my Lord:
    My goodness is nothing without thee;
But in the saints that are in the earth,
    And in the excellent, in them is all my delight.
Their sorrows shall be multiplied that hasten after another god:
Their drink offerings of blood will I not offer,
    Nor take up their names into my lips.
The Lord is the portion of mine inheritance and of my cup:

    Thou maintainest my lot.
The lines are fallen unto me in pleasant places;
    Yea, I have a goodly heritage.
I will bless the Lord, who hath given me counsel:
    My reins also instruct me in the night seasons.
I have set the Lord always before me:
    Because he is at my right hand, I shall not be moved.
Therefore my heart is glad, and my glory rejoiceth;
    My flesh also shall rest in hope.
For thou wilt not leave my soul in hell;
    Neither wilt thou suffer thine Holy One to see corruption.
Thou wilt show me the path of life:
In thy presence is fulness of joy;
    At thy right hand there are pleasures for evermore.

PSALM XVIII.

I will love thee, O Lord, my strength.
    The Lord is my rock, and my fortress, and my deliverer;
My God, my strength, in whom I will trust;
    My buckler, and the horn of my salvation, and my high tower.
I will call upon the Lord, who is worthy to be praised:
    So shall I be saved from mine enemies.
The sorrows of death compassed me,
    And the floods of ungodly men made me afraid.
The sorrows of hell compassed me about:

The snares of death prevented me.
In my distress I called upon the Lord,
  And cried unto my God:
He heard my voice out of his temple,
  And my cry came before him, even into his
    ears.
Then the earth shook and trembled;
The foundations also of the hills moved
  And were shaken, because he was wroth.
There went up a smoke out of his nostrils,
And fire out of his mouth devoured:
  Coals were kindled by it.
He bowed the heavens also, and came down:
  And darkness was under his feet.
And he rode upon a cherub, and did fly;
  Yea, he did fly upon the wings of the wind.
He made darkness his secret place;
His pavilion round about him
  Were dark waters and thick clouds of the skies.
With the merciful thou wilt show thyself merciful;
  With an upright man thou wilt show thyself
    upright;
With the pure thou wilt show thyself pure;
  And with the froward thou wilt show thyself
    froward.
For thou wilt save the afflicted people;
  But wilt bring down high looks.
For thou wilt light my candle:
  The Lord my God will enlighten my darkness.
For by thee I have run through a troop:
  And by my God have I leaped over a wall.
As for God, his way is perfect:
The word of the Lord is tried:

He is a buckler to all those that trust in him.
For who is God save the Lord?
Or who is a rock save our God?
It is God that girdeth me with strength,
And maketh my way perfect.
Thou hast also given me the shield of thy salvation:
And thy right hand hath holden me up,
And thy gentleness hath made me great.
Thou hast enlarged my steps under me,
That my feet did not slip.
The Lord liveth; and blessed be my rock;
And let the God of my salvation be exalted.
It is God that avengeth me,
And subdueth the people under me.
He delivereth me from mine enemies:
Yea, thou liftest me up above those that rise up against me:
Thou hast delivered me from the violent man.
Therefore will I give thanks unto thee, O Lord, among the heathen,
And sing praises unto thy name.

PSALM XIX.

The heavens declare the glory of God;
And the firmament showeth his handywork.
Day unto day uttereth speech,
And night unto night showeth knowledge.
There is no speech nor language,
And their voice is not heard.
Their sound is gone out through all the earth,
And their words to the end of the world.

In them hath he set a tabernacle for the sun,
Which is as a bridegroom coming out of his chamber,
    And rejoiceth as a strong man to run a race.
His going forth is from the end of the heaven,
And his circuit unto the ends of it:
    And there is nothing hid from the heat thereof.
The law of the Lord is perfect, converting the soul:
    The testimony of the Lord is sure, making wise the simple.
The statutes of the Lord are right, rejoicing the heart:
    The commandment of the Lord is pure, enlightening the eyes.
The fear of the Lord is clean, enduring forever:
    The judgments of the Lord are true and righteous altogether:
More to be desired are they than gold, yea, than much fine gold:
    Sweeter also than honey and the honeycomb.
Moreover, by them is thy servant warned:
    And in keeping of them there is great reward.
Who can understand his errors?
    Cleanse thou me from secret faults.
Keep back thy servant also from presumptuous sins;
Let them not have dominion over me: then shall I be upright.
    And I shall be innocent from the great transgression.
Let the words of my mouth,
    And the meditation of my heart,
Be acceptable in thy sight,
    O Lord, my strength and my redeemer.

PSALM XXII

My God, my God, why hast thou forsaken me?
 Why art thou so far from helping me, and from
  the words of my complaining?
O my God, I cry in the daytime, but thou hearest
 not;
 And in the night season, and am not silent.
But thou art holy,
 O thou that inhabitest the praises of Israel.
Our fathers trusted in thee:
 They trusted, and thou didst deliver them.
They cried unto thee, and were delivered:
 They trusted in thee, and were not confounded.
But I am a worm, and no man;
 A reproach of men, and despised of the people.
All they that see me laugh me to scorn;
 They shoot out the lip, they shake the head,
  saying,
He trusted on the Lord that he would deliver him:
 Let him deliver him, seeing he delighted in him.
The assembly of the wicked have inclosed me:
 They pierced my hands and my feet.
I may tell all my bones:
 They look and stare upon me.
They part my garments among them,
 And cast lots upon my vesture.
But be not thou far from me, O Lord:
 O my strength, haste thee to help me.
Deliver my soul from the sword;
 My blood from the power of the dog.
Save me from the lion's mouth:

For thou hast heard me from the horns of the
   unicorns.
I will declare thy name unto my brethren:
   In the midst of the congregation will I praise
      thee.
Ye that fear the Lord, praise him;
All ye the seed of Jacob, glorify him;
   And fear him, all ye the seed of Israel.
For he hath not despised nor abhorred the affliction
   of the afflicted;
Neither hath he hid his face from him;
   But when he cried unto him, he heard.
My praise shall be of thee in the great congregation:
   I will pay my vows before them that fear him.
The meek shall eat and be satisfied:
They shall praise the Lord that seek him:
   Your heart shall live forever.
All the ends of the world shall remember and turn
   unto the Lord:
   And all the kindreds of the nations shall wor-
      ship before thee.
For the kingdom is the Lord's:
   And he is the governor among the nations.
A seed shall serve him;
   It shall be accounted to the Lord for a genera-
      tion.
They shall come, and shall declare his righteousness
   Unto a people that shall be born that he hath
      done this.

PSALM XXIII.

The Lord is my shepherd;
    I shall not want.
He maketh me to lie down in green pastures:
    He leadeth me beside the still waters.
He restoreth my soul,
    He leadeth me in the paths of righteousness for his name's sake.
Yea, though I walk through the valley of the shadow of death,
I will fear no evil: for thou art with me;
    Thy rod and thy staff they comfort me.
Thou preparest a table before me in the presence of mine enemies:
    Thou anointest my head with oil; my cup runneth over.
Surely goodness and mercy shall follow me all the days of my life:
    And I will dwell in the house of the Lord for ever.

PSALM XXIV.

The earth is the Lord's, and the fulness thereof;
    The world, and they that dwell therein.
For he hath founded it upon the seas,
    And established it upon the floods.
Who shall ascend into the hill of the Lord?
    Or who shall stand in his holy place?
He that hath clean hands, and a pure heart;
    Who hath not lifted up his soul unto vanity, nor sworn deceitfully.

He shall receive the blessing from the Lord,
>And righteousness from the God of his salvation.

This is the generation of them that seek him,
>That seek thy face, O Jacob.

Lift up your heads, O ye gates;
And be ye lifted up, ye everlasting doors;
>And the King of glory shall come in.

Who is this King of glory?
The Lord strong and mighty,
>The Lord mighty in battle.

Lift up your heads, O ye gates;
Even lift them up, ye everlasting doors:
>And the King of glory shall come in.

Who is this King of glory?
The Lord of hosts,
>He is the King of glory.

PSALM XXV.

Unto thee, O Lord, do I lift up my soul.
O my God, I trust in thee: let me not be ashamed,
>Let not mine enemies triumph over me.

Yea, let none that wait on thee be ashamed:
>Let them be ashamed which transgress without cause.

Show me thy ways, O Lord;
>Teach me thy paths.

Lead me in thy truth, and teach me:
For thou art the God of my salvation;
>On thee do I wait all the day.

Remember, O Lord, thy tender mercies and thy loving-kindnesses;

  For they have been ever of old.
Remember not the sins of my youth, nor my transgressions:
According to thy mercy remember thou me,
  For thy goodness' sake, O Lord.
Good and upright is the Lord:
  Therefore will he teach sinners in the way.
The meek will he guide in judgment:
  And the meek will he teach his way.
All the paths of the Lord are mercy and truth
  Unto such as keep his covenant and his testimonies.
For thy name's sake, O Lord,
  Pardon mine iniquity; for it is great.
What man is he that feareth the Lord?
  Him shall he teach in the way that he shall choose.
His soul shall dwell at ease;
  And his seed shall inherit the earth.
The secret of the Lord is with them that fear him;
  And he will show them his covenant.
Mine eyes are ever toward the Lord;
  For he shall pluck my feet out of the net.
Turn thee unto me, and have mercy upon me;
  For I am desolate and afflicted.
The troubles of my heart are enlarged:
  O bring thou me out of my distresses.
Look upon mine affliction and my pain;
  And forgive all my sins.
Consider mine enemies; for they are many;
  And they hate me with cruel hatred.
O keep my soul, and deliver me:
  Let me not be ashamed; for I put my trust in thee

Let integrity and uprightness preserve me;
　For I wait on thee.
Redeem Israel, O God,
　Out of all his troubles.

PSALM XXVII.

The Lord is my light and my salvation; whom
shall I fear?
　The Lord is the strength of my life; of whom
　　shall I be afraid?
Though an host should encamp against me,
　My heart shall not fear:
Though war should rise against me,
　In this will I be confident.
One thing have I desired of the Lord, that will I
seek after;
　That I may dwell in the house of the Lord all
　　the days of my life,
To behold the beauty of the Lord,
　And to inquire in his temple.
For in the time of trouble he shall hide me in his
pavilion:
In the secret of his tabernacle shall he hide me;
　He shall set me up upon a rock.
Therefore will I offer in his tabernacle sacrifices of
joy;
　I will sing, yea, I will sing praises unto the
　　Lord.
Hear, O Lord, when I cry with my voice:
　Have mercy also upon me, and answer me.
When thou saidst, seek ye my face;

My heart said unto thee, Thy face, Lord, will
I seek.
Hide not thy face far from me;
Put not thy servant away in anger;
Thou hast been my help;
Leave me not, neither forsake me, O God of
my salvation.
When my father and my mother forsake me,
Then the Lord will take me up.
I had fainted, unless I had believed to see the goodness of the Lord
In the land of the living.
Wait on the Lord:
Be of good courage, and he shall strengthen thine
heart:
Wait, I say, on the Lord.

PSALM XXIX.

Give unto the Lord, O ye mighty,
Give unto the Lord glory and strength.
Give unto the Lord the glory due unto his name;
Worship the Lord in the beauty of holiness.
The voice of the Lord is upon the waters:
The God of glory thundereth:
The Lord is upon many waters.
The voice of the Lord is powerful;
The voice of the Lord is full of majesty.
The voice of the Lord breaketh the cedars;
Yes, the Lord breaketh the cedars of Lebanon.
He maketh them also to skip like a calf;
Lebanon and Sirion like a young unicorn.
The voice of the Lord divideth the flames of fire.

The voice of the Lord shaketh the wilderness;
> The Lord shaketh the wilderness of Kadesh.

The Lord sitteth upon the flood;
> Yea, the Lord sitteth King for ever.

The Lord will give strength unto his people;
> The Lord will bless his people with peace.

PSALM XXX.

I WILL extol thee, O Lord; for thou hast lifted me up,
> And hast not made my foes to rejoice over me.

O Lord my God,
> I cried unto thee, and thou hast healed me.

O Lord, thou hast brought up my soul from the grave:
> Thou hast kept me alive, that I should not go down to the pit:

Sing unto the Lord, O ye saints of his,
> And give thanks at the remembrance of his holiness.

For his anger endureth but a moment; in his favor is life:
> Weeping may endure for a night, but joy cometh in the morning.

And in my prosperity I said,
> I shall never be moved.

Lord, by thy favor thou hast made my mountain to stand strong:
> Thou didst hide thy face, and I was troubled.

I cried to thee, O Lord;
> And unto the Lord I made supplication.

What profit is there in my blood, when I go down
  to the pit?
    Shall the dust praise thee? shall it declare thy
      truth?
Hear, O Lord, and have mercy upon me:
  Lord, be thou my helper.
Thou hast turned for me my mourning into dancing:
  Thou hast put off my sackcloth, and girded me
    with gladness;
To the end that I may sing praise to thee, and not
  be silent.
    O Lord my God, I will give thanks unto thee
      for ever.

PSALM XXXI.

In thee, O Lord, do I put my trust;
Let me never be ashamed:
  Deliver me in thy righteousness.
Bow down thine ear to me; deliver me speedily:
Be thou my strong rock,
  For an house of defence to save me.
For thou art my rock and my fortress;
  Therefore for thy name's sake lead me, and
    guide me.
Pull me out of the net that they have laid privily
  for me:
  For thou art my strength.
Into thine hand I commit my spirit:
  Thou hast redeemed me, O Lord God of truth.
I have hated them that regard lying vanities:
  But I trust in the Lord.
I will be glad and rejoice in thy mercy:

For thou hast considered my trouble;
  Thou hast known my soul in adversities;
Oh how great is thy goodness, which thou hast laid up for them that fear thee;
  Which thou hast wrought for them that trust in thee before the sons of men!
Thou shalt hide them in the secret of thy presence from the pride of man:
  Thou shalt keep them secretly in a pavilion from the strife of tongues.
Blessed be the Lord:
  For he hath showed me his marvellous kindness in a strong city.
For I said in my haste,
  I am cut off from before thine eyes:
Nevertheless thou heardest the voice of my supplications
  When I cried unto thee.
O love the Lord, all ye his saints:
For the Lord preserveth the faithful,
  And plentifully rewardeth the proud-doer.
Be of good courage, and he shall strengthen your heart,
  All ye that hope in the Lord.

PSALM XXXIII.

Rejoice in the Lord, O ye righteous:
  For praise is comely for the upright.
Praise the Lord with harp:
  Sing unto him with the psaltery and an instrument of ten strings.

Sing unto him a new song:
> Play skilfully with a loud noise.

For the word of the Lord is right;
> And all his works are done in truth.

He loveth righteousness and judgment.
> The earth is full of the goodness of the Lord.

By the word of the Lord were the heavens made;
> And all the host of them by the breath of his mouth.

He gathereth the waters of the sea together as an heap:
> He layeth up the depth in storehouses.

Let all the earth fear the Lord:
> Let all the inhabitants of the world stand in awe of him.

For he spake, and it was done;
> He commanded, and it stood fast.

The Lord bringeth the counsel of the heathen to naught:
> He maketh the devices of the people of none effect.

The counsel of the Lord standeth for ever,
> The thoughts of his heart to all generations.

Blessed is the nation whose God is the Lord;
> And the people whom he hath chosen for his own inheritance.

The Lord looketh from heaven;
> He beholdeth all the sons of men.

From the place of his habitation he looketh
> Upon all the inhabitants of the earth.

He fashioneth their hearts alike;
> He considereth all their works.

There is no king saved by the multitude of an host:

A mighty man is not delivered by much
    strength.
An horse is a vain thing for safety:
    Neither shall he deliver any by his great
        strength.
Behold the eye of the Lord is upon them that fear
    him,
    Upon them that hope in his mercy;
To deliver their soul from death,
    And to keep them alive in famine.
Our soul waiteth for the Lord:
    He is our help and our shield.
For our heart shall rejoice in him,
    Because we have trusted in his holy name.
Let thy mercy, O Lord, be upon us,
    According as we hope in thee.

PSALM XXXIV.

I WILL bless the Lord at all times:
    His praise shall continually be in my mouth.
My soul shall make her boast in the Lord:
    The humble shall hear thereof, and be glad.
O magnify the Lord with me,
    And let us exalt his name together.
I sought the Lord, and he heard me,
    And delivered me from all my fears.
They looked unto him, and were lightened:
    And their faces were not ashamed.
This poor man cried, and the Lord heard him,
    And saved him out of all his troubles.
The angel of the Lord encampeth round about them
    that fear him,

And delivereth them.
O taste and see that the Lord is good:
　　Blessed is the man that trusteth in him.
O fear the Lord, ye his saints:
　　For there is no want to them that fear him.
The young lions do lack, and suffer hunger:
　　But they that seek the Lord shall not want any good thing.
Come, ye children, hearken unto me:
　　I will teach you the fear of the Lord.
What man is he that desireth life,
　　And loveth many days, that he may see good?
Keep thy tongue from evil,
　　And thy lips from speaking guile.
Depart from evil, and do good;
　　Seek peace, and pursue it.
The eyes of the Lord are upon the righteous,
　　And his ears are open unto their cry.
The face of the Lord is against them that do evil,
　　To cut off the remembrance of them from the earth.
The righteous cry, and the Lord heareth,
　　And delivereth them out of all their troubles.
The Lord is nigh unto them that are of a broken heart;
　　And saveth such as be of a contrite spirit.
Many are the afflictions of the righteous:
　　But the Lord delivereth him out of them all.
He keepeth all his bones:
　　Not one of them is broken.
Evil shall slay the wicked:
　　And they that hate the righteous shall be desolate.

The Lord redeemeth the soul of his servants:
> And none of them that trust in him shall be desolate.

PSALM XXXVI.

The transgression of the wicked saith within my heart,
> That there is no fear of God before his eyes.

For he flattereth himself in his own eyes,
> Until his iniquity be found to be hateful.

The words of his mouth are iniquity and deceit:
> He hath left off to be wise, and to do good.

He deviseth mischief upon his bed:
He setteth himself in a way that is not good;
> He abhorreth not evil.

Thy mercy, O Lord, is in the heavens;
> And thy faithfulness reacheth unto the clouds.

Thy righteousness is like the great mountains;
> Thy judgments are a great deep:

O Lord, thou preservest man and beast.
How excellent is thy loving-kindness, O God!
> Therefore the children of men put their trust under the shadow of thy wings.

They shall be abundantly satisfied with the fatness of thy house:
> And thou shalt make them drink of the river of thy pleasures.

For with thee is the fountain of life:
> In thy light shall we see light.

O continue thy loving-kindness unto them that know thee;
> And thy righteousness to the upright in heart.

Let not the foot of pride come against me;
> And let not the hand of the wicked remove me.

There are the workers of iniquity fallen:
> They are cast down, and shall not be able to rise.

PSALM XXXVII.

Fret not thyself because of evil-doers,
> Neither be thou envious against the workers of iniquity.

For they shall soon be cut down like the grass,
> And wither as the green herb.

Trust in the Lord, and do good;
> So shalt thou dwell in the land, and verily thou shalt be fed.

Delight thyself also in the Lord;
> And he shall give thee the desires of thine heart.

Commit thy way unto the Lord:
> Trust also in him; and he shall bring it to pass.

And he shall bring forth thy righteousness as the light,
> And thy judgment as the noonday.

Rest in the Lord, and wait patiently for him:
Fret not thyself because of him who prospereth in his way,
> Because of the man who bringeth wicked devices to pass.

Cease from anger, and forsake wrath:
> Fret not thyself in any wise to do evil.

For evil-doers shall be cut off:
> But those that wait upon the Lord, they shall inherit the earth.

For yet a little while, and the wicked shall not be:
> Yea, thou shalt diligently consider his place,
> and it shall not be:

But the meek shall inherit the earth;
> And shall delight themselves in the abundance
> of peace.

The wicked plotteth against the just,
> And gnasheth upon him with his teeth.

The Lord shall laugh at him:
> For he seeth that his day is coming.

The wicked have drawn out the sword, and have bent their bow,
To cast down the poor and needy,
> And to slay such as be of upright conversation.

Their sword shall enter into their own heart,
> And their bows shall be broken.

A little that the righteous man hath is better
> Than the riches of many wicked.

For the arms of the wicked shall be broken:
> But the Lord upholdeth the righteous.

The Lord knoweth the days of the upright:
> And their inheritance shall be for ever.

They shall not be ashamed in the evil time:
> And in the days of famine they shall be satisfied.

The steps of a good man are ordered by the Lord:
> And he delighteth in his way.

Though he fall, he shall not be utterly cast down:
> For the Lord upholdeth him with his hand.

I have been young, and now am old;
Yet have I not seen the righteous forsake·
> Nor his seed begging bread.

He is ever merciful, and lendeth;
> And his seed is blessed.

Depart from evil, and do good:
> And dwell for evermore.
For the Lord loveth judgment,
> And forsaketh not his saints;
They are preserved for ever:
> But the seed of the wicked shall be cut off.
The righteous shall inherit the land,
> And dwell therein for ever.
The mouth of the righteous speaketh wisdom,
> And his tongue talketh of judgment.
The law of his God is in his heart;
> None of his steps shall slide.
The wicked watcheth the righteous,
> And seeketh to slay him.
The Lord will not leave him in his hand,
> Nor condemn him when he is judged.
Wait on the Lord, and keep his way,
And he shall exalt thee to inherit the land:
> When the wicked are cut off, thou shalt see it.
I have seen the wicked in great power,
> And spreading himself like a green bay-tree.
Yet he passed away, and, lo, he was not:
> Yea, I sought him, but he could not be found.
Mark the perfect man, and behold the upright:
> For the end of that man is peace.
But the transgressors shall be destroyed together:
> The end of the wicked shall be cut off.
But the salvation of the righteous is of the Lord:
> He is their strength in the time of trouble.
And the Lord shall help them, and deliver them:
He shall deliver them from the wicked, and save them,
> Because they trust in him.

PSALM XXXIX.

I said, I will take heed to my ways,
    That I sin not with my tongue:
I will keep my mouth with a bridle,
    While the wicked is before me.
I was dumb with silence, I held my peace, even from good;
    And my sorrow was stirred.
My heart was hot within me,
While I was musing the fire burned:
    Then spake I with my tongue,
Lord, make me to know mine end,
And the measure of my days, what it is;
    That I may know how frail I am.
Behold, thou hast made my days as an handbreadth;
And mine age is as nothing before thee:
    Verily every man at his best state is altogether vanity.
Surely every man walketh in a vain show:
Surely they are disquieted in vain:
    He heapeth up riches, and knoweth not who shall gather them.
And now, Lord, what wait I for?
    My hope is in thee.
Deliver me from all my transgressions:
    Make me not the reproach of the foolish.
I was dumb, I opened not my mouth·
    Because thou didst it.
Remove thy stroke away from me:
    I am consumed by the blow of thine hand.
When thou with rebukes dost correct man for iniquity,

Thou makest his beauty to consume away like a moth:
    Surely every man is vanity.
Hear my prayer, O Lord,
And give ear unto my cry;
    Hold not thy peace at my tears:
For I am a stranger with thee,
    And a sojourner, as all my fathers were.
O spare me, that I may recover strength,
    Before I go hence, and be no more.

PSALM XL.

I WAITED patiently for the Lord;
    And he inclined unto me, and heard my cry.
He brought me up also out of an horrible pit, out of the miry clay,
    And set my feet upon a rock, and established my goings.
And he hath put a new song in my mouth,
    Even praise unto our God:
Many shall see it, and fear,
    And shall trust in the Lord.
Blessed is that man
That maketh the Lord his trust,
    And respecteth not the proud, nor such as turn aside to lies.
Many, O Lord my God, are thy wonderful works which thou hast done,
    And thy thoughts which are to us-ward:
They cannot be reckoned up in order unto thee:
    If I would declare and speak of them, they are more than can be numbered.

Sacrifice and offering thou didst not desire;
Mine ears hast thou opened:
    Burnt-offering and sin-offering hast thou not
        required.
Then said I, Lo, I come:
    In the volume of the book it is written of me.
I delight to do thy will, O my God:
    Yea, thy law is within my heart.
I have preached righteousness in the great congregation:
Lo, I have not refrained my lips,
    O Lord, thou knowest.
I have not hid thy righteousness within my heart;
I have declared thy faithfulness and thy salvation:
    I have not concealed thy loving-kindness and
        thy truth from the great congregation.
Withhold not thou thy tender mercies from me, O Lord:
    Let thy loving-kindness and thy truth continually preserve me.
For innumerable evils have compassed me about:
    Mine iniquities have taken hold upon me, so
        that I am not able to look up;
They are more than the hairs of mine head:
    Therefore my heart faileth me.
Be pleased, O Lord, to deliver me:
    O Lord, make haste to help me.
Let all those that seek thee rejoice and be glad in thee:
    Let such as love thy salvation say continually,
        Lord be magnified.
But I am poor and needy; yet the Lord thinketh upon me:

Thou art my help and my deliverer;
　Make no tarrying, O my God.

PSALM XLII.

As the hart panteth after the water-brooks,
　So panteth my soul after thee, O God.
My soul thirsteth for God, for the living God:
　When shall I come and appear before God!
My tears have been my meat day and night,
　While they continually say unto me, Where is thy God?
When I remember these things, I pour out my soul in me:
　For I had gone with the multitude,
I went with them to the house of God,
　With the voice of joy and praise, with a multitude that kept holyday.
Why art thou cast down, O my soul?
　And why art thou disquieted in me?
Hope thou in God: for I shall yet praise him
　For his presence is salvation.
O my God, my soul is cast down within me:
　Therefore will I remember thee.
Deep calleth unto deep at the noise of thy waterspouts;
　All thy waves and thy billows are gone over me.
Yet the Lord will command his loving-kindness in the daytime,
And in the night his song shall be with me,
　And my prayer unto the God of my life.
I will say unto God my rock, Why hast thou forgotten me?

Why go I mourning because of the oppression
of the enemy?
As with a sword in my bones, mine enemies reproach me;
   While they say daily unto me, Where is thy
God?
Why art thou cast down, O my soul?
   And why art thou disquieted within me?
Hope thou in God: for I shall yet praise him,
   Who is the health of my countenance, and my
God.

PSALM XLVI.

God is our refuge and strength,
   A very present help in trouble.
Therefore will not we fear, though the earth be removed,
   And though the mountains be carried into the
midst of the sea;
Though the waters thereof roar and be troubled,
   Though the mountains shake with the swelling
thereof.
There is a river, the streams whereof shall make glad
the city of God,
   The holy place of the tabernacles of the Most
High.
God is in the midst of her; she shall not be moved;
   God shall help her, and that right early.
The heathen raged, the kingdoms were moved:
   He uttered his voice, the earth melted.
The Lord of hosts is with us;
   The God of Jacob is our refuge.

Come, behold the works of the Lord,
    What desolations he hath made in the earth.
He maketh wars to cease unto the end of the earth;
He breaketh the bow, and cutteth the spear in sunder;
    He burneth the chariot in the fire.
Be still, and know that I am God:
    I will be exalted among the heathen,
I will be exalted in the earth.
The Lord of hosts is with us;
    The God of Jacob is our refuge.

PSALM XLVII.

O clap your hands, all ye people;
    Shout unto God with the voice of triumph.
For the Lord most high is terrible;
    He is a great King over all the earth.
He shall subdue the people under us,
    And the nations under our feet.
He shall choose our inheritance for us,
    The excellency of Jacob whom he loved.
God is gone up with a shout,
    The Lord with the sound of a trumpet.
Sing praises to God, sing praises:
    Sing praises unto our King, sing praises.
For God is the King of all the earth:
    Sing ye praises with understanding.
God reigneth over the heathen:
    God sitteth upon the throne of his holiness.
The princes of the people are gathered together,
    Even the people of the God of Abraham:
For the shields of the earth belong unto God:
    He is greatly exalted.

PSALM XLVIII.

Great is the Lord, and greatly to be praised
    In the city of our God, in the mountain of his holiness.
Beautiful for situation, the joy of the whole earth,
    Is mount Zion, on the sides of the north,
The city of the great King.
    God is known in her palaces for a refuge.
As we have heard, so have we seen
In the city of the Lord of hosts, in the city of our God:
    God will establish it for ever.
We have thought of thy loving-kindness, O God,
    In the midst of thy temple.
According to thy name, O God,
So is thy praise unto the ends of the earth;
    Thy right hand is full of righteousness.
Let mount Zion rejoice,
Let the daughters of Judah be glad,
    Because of thy judgments.
Walk about Zion, and go round about her:
    Tell the towers thereof.
Mark ye well her bulwarks,
Consider her palaces;
    That ye may tell it to the generation following:
For this God is our God for ever and ever:
    He will be our guide even unto death.

PSALM XLIX.

Hear this, all ye people;
    Give ear, all ye inhabitants of the world:
Both low and high,
    Rich and poor, together.
My mouth shall speak of wisdom;
    And the meditation of my heart shall be of understanding.
I will incline mine ear to a parable:
    I will open my dark saying upon the harp.
Wherefore should I fear in the days of evil,
    When the iniquity of my heels shall compass me about?
They that trust in their wealth,
    And boast themselves in the multitude of their riches;
None of them can by any means redeem his brother,
    Nor give to God a ransom for him:
(For the redemption of their soul is precious,
    And it ceaseth forever:)
That he should still live forever,
    And not see corruption:
For he seeth that wise men die,
Likewise the fool and the brutish person perish,
    And leave their wealth to others.
Their inward thought is, that their houses shall continue for ever,
And their dwelling-places to all generations;
    They call their lands after their own names.
Nevertheless man being in honor abideth not:
    He is like the beasts that perish.

This their way is their folly.
　　Yet their posterity approve their sayings;
Like sheep they are laid in the grave;
　　Death shall feed on them;
And the upright shall have dominion over them in the morning;
　　And their beauty shall consume in the grave from their dwelling.
But God will redeem my soul from the power of the grave:
　　For he shall receive me.
Be not thou afraid when one is made rich,
　　When the glory of his house is increased;
For when he dieth he shall carry nothing away.
　　His glory shall not descend after him.
Though while he lived he blessed his soul:
　　And men will praise thee, when thou doest well to thyself.
He shall go to the generation of his fathers;
　　They shall never see light.
Man that is in honor, and understandeth not,
　　Is like the beasts that perish.

PSALM L.

The mighty God, even the Lord, hath spoken,
And called the earth
　　From the rising of the sun unto the going down thereof.
Out of Zion, the perfection of beauty,
　　God hath shined.
Our God shall come, and shall not keep silence:
A fire shall devour before him,

And it shall be very tempestuous round about
    him.
He shall call to the heavens from above,
    And to the earth, that he may judge his people.
Gather my saints together unto me;
    Those that have made a covenant with me by
        sacrifice.
And the heavens shall declare his righteousness:
    For God is judge himself.
Hear, O my people, and I will speak;
O Israel, and I will testify against thee:
    I am God, even thy God.
I will not reprove thee for thy sacrifices,
    Or thy burnt offerings, to have been continu-
        ally before me.
I will take no bullock out of thy house,
    Nor he-goats out of thy folds.
For every beast of the forest is mine,
    And the cattle upon a thousand hills.
I know all the fowls of the mountains:
    And the wild beasts of the field are mine.
If I were hungry, I would not tell thee:
    For the world is mine, and the fulness thereof.
Will I eat the flesh of bulls,
    Or drink the blood of goats?
Offer unto God thanksgiving;
    And pay thy vows unto the Most High;
And call upon me in the day of trouble:
    I will deliver thee, and thou shalt glorify me.
Whoso offereth praise glorifieth me:
And to him that ordereth his conversation aright
    Will I show the salvation of God.

PSALM LI.

Have mercy upon me, O God, according to thy loving-kindness:
    According unto the multitude of thy tender mercies, blot out my transgressions.
Wash me thoroughly from mine iniquity,
    And cleanse me from my sin.
For I acknowledge my transgressions:
    And my sin is ever before me.
Against thee, thee only, have I sinned,
    And done this evil in thy sight:
That thou mightest be justified when thou speakest,
    And be clear when thou judgest.
Behold I was shapen in iniquity;
    And in sin did my mother conceive me.
Behold, thou desirest truth in the inward parts:
    And in the hidden part thou shalt make me to know wisdom.
Purge me with hyssop, and I shall be clean:
    Wash me, and I shall be whiter than snow.
Make me to hear joy and gladness;
    That the bones which thou hast broken may rejoice.
Hide thy face from my sins,
    And blot out all mine iniquities.
Create in me a clean heart, O God;
    And renew a right spirit within me.
Cast me not away from thy presence;
    And take not thy Holy Spirit from me.
Restore unto me the joy of thy salvation;
    And uphold me with thy free Spirit.

Then will I teach transgressors thy ways;
    And sinners shall be converted unto thee.
Deliver me from blood-guiltiness, O God,
Thou God of my salvation:
    And my tongue shall sing aloud of thy righteousness.
O Lord, open thou my lips;
    And my mouth shall show forth thy praise.
For thou desirest not sacrifice; else would I give it:
    Thou delightest not in burnt-offering.
The sacrifices of God are a broken spirit:
    A broken and a contrite heart, O God, thou wilt not despise.

PSALM LVII.

Be merciful unto me, O God, be merciful unto me:
    For my soul trusteth in thee:
Yea, in the shadow of thy wings will I make my refuge,
    Until these calamities be overpast.
I will cry unto God Most High;
    Unto God that performeth all things for me.
He shall send from heaven, and save me
From the reproach of him that would swallow me up.
    God shall send forth his mercy and his truth.
Be thou exalted, O God, above the heavens;
    Let thy glory be above all the earth.
My heart is fixed, O God, my heart is fixed:
    I will sing and give praise.
Awake up, my glory; awake, psaltery and harp:
    I myself will awake early.
I will praise thee, O Lord, among the people:

I will sing unto thee among the nations.
For thy mercy is great unto the heavens,
    And thy truth unto the clouds.
Be thou exalted, O God, above the heavens:
    Let thy glory be above all the earth.

PSALM LXII.

Truly my soul waiteth upon God:
    From him cometh my salvation.
He only is my rock and my salvation;
    He is my defence; I shall not be greatly moved.
My soul, wait thou only upon God;
    For my expectation is from him.
He only is my rock and my salvation:
    He is my defence; I shall not be moved.
In God is my salvation and my glory;
    The rock of my strength, and my refuge, is in God.
Trust in him at all times; ye people,
Pour out your heart before him:
    God is a refuge for us.
Surely men of low degree are vanity, and men of high degree are a lie:
To be laid in the balance,
    They are altogether lighter than vanity.
Trust not in oppression,
And become not vain in robbery:
    If riches increase, set not your heart upon them.
God hath spoken once;
Twice have I heard this;
    That power belongeth unto God.

Also unto thee, O Lord, belongeth mercy:
>For thou renderest to every man according to his work.

PSALM LXIII.

O God, thou art my God; early will I seek thee:
>My soul thirsteth for thee,

My flesh longeth for thee,
>In a dry and thirsty land, where no water is;

To see thy power and thy glory,
>So as I have seen thee in the sanctuary.

Because thy loving-kindness is better than life;
>My lips shall praise thee.

Thus will I bless thee while I live:
>I will lift up my hands in thy name.

My soul shall be satisfied as with marrow and fatness;
>And my mouth shall praise thee with joyful lips:

When I remember thee upon my bed,
>And meditate on thee in the night watches.

Because thou hast been my help,
>Therefore in the shadow of thy wings will I rejoice.

My soul followeth hard after thee:
>Thy right hand upholdeth me.

PSALM LXV.

Praise waiteth for thee, O God, in Sion:
>And unto thee shall the vow be performed.

O thou that hearest prayer,
>Unto thee shall all flesh come.

Iniquities prevail against me:

As for our transgressions, thou shalt purge them away.
Blessed is the man whom thou choosest, and causest to approach unto thee,
That he may dwell in thy courts:
We shall be satisfied with the goodness of thy house,
Even of thy holy temple.
By terrible things in righteousness wilt thou answer us,
O God of our salvation;
Who art the confidence of all the ends of the earth,
And of them that are afar off upon the sea:
Which by his strength setteth fast the mountains;
Being girded with power:
Which stilleth the noise of the seas, the noise of their waves,
And the tumult of the people.
They also that dwell in the uttermost parts are afraid at thy tokens.
Thou makest the outgoings of the morning and evening to rejoice.
Thou visitest the earth, and waterest it:
Thou greatly enrichest it
With the river of God, which is full of water:
Thou preparest them corn, when thou hast so provided for it.
Thou waterest the ridges thereof abundantly: thou settlest the furrows thereof:
Thou makest it soft with showers: thou blessest the springing thereof.
Thou crownest the year with thy goodness;
And thy paths drop fatness.
They drop upon the pastures of the wilderness·

And the little hills rejoice on every side.
The pastures are clothed with flocks;
The valleys also are covered over with corn:
　　They shout for joy, they also sing.

PSALM LXVI.

MAKE a joyful noise unto God, all ye lands:
Sing forth the honor of his name:
　　Make his praise glorious.
Say unto God, How terrible art thou in thy works!
　　Through the greatness of thy power shall thine
　　　　enemies submit themselves unto thee.
All the earth shall worship thee,
And shall sing unto thee;
　　They shall sing to thy name.
Come and see the works of God!
　　He is terrible in his doing toward the children
　　　　of men.
He turned the sea into dry land:
They went through the flood on foot:
　　There did we rejoice in him.
He ruleth by his power for ever;
His eyes behold the nations:
　　Let not the rebellious exalt themselves.
O bless our God, ye people,
　　And make the voice of his praise to be heard:
Which holdeth our soul in life,
　　And suffereth not our feet to be moved.
For thou, O God, hast proved us:
　　Thou hast tried us, as silver is tried.
Thou broughtest us into the net;

Thou laidst affliction upon our loins.
Thou hast caused men to ride over our heads;
We went through fire and through water;
> But thou broughtest us out into a wealthy place.

Come and hear, all ye that fear God, and I will declare
> What he hath done for my soul.

I cried unto him with my mouth,
> And he was extolled with my tongue.

If I regard iniquity in my heart,
> The Lord will not hear me:

But verily God hath heard me;
> He hath attended to the voice of my prayer.

Blessed be God,
> Which hath not turned away my prayer, nor his mercy from me.

PSALM LXVII.

God be merciful unto us, and bless us;
> And cause his face to shine upon us.

That thy way may be known upon earth,
> Thy saving health among all nations.

Let the people praise thee, O God;
> Let all the people praise thee.

O let the nations be glad and sing for joy:
For thou shalt judge the people righteously,
> And govern the nations upon earth.

Let the people praise thee, O God;
> Let all the people praise thee.

Then shall the earth yield her increase;
> And God, even our own God, shall bless us.

God shall bless us;
> And all the ends of the earth shall fear him.

PSALM LXVIII.

Let God arise, let his enemies be scattered:
> Let them also that hate him flee before him.

As smoke is driven away, so drive them away:
As wax melteth before the fire,
> So let the wicked perish at the presence of God.

But let the righteous be glad; let them rejoice before God:
> Yea, let them exceedingly rejoice.

Sing unto God, sing praises to his name:
Extol him that rideth upon the heavens
> By his name JAH, and rejoice before him.

A father of the fatherless, and a judge of the widows,
> Is God in his holy habitation.

God setteth the solitary in families:
He bringeth out those which are bound with chains:
> But the rebellious dwell in a dry land.

O God, when thou wentest forth before thy people,
> When thou didst march through the wilderness;

The earth shook,
The heavens also dropped at the presence of God:
> Even Sinai itself was moved at the presence of God, the God of Israel.

Thou, O God, didst send a plentiful rain,
> Whereby thou didst confirm thine inheritance when it was weary.

Thy congregation hath dwelt therein:
> Thou, O God, hast prepared of thy goodness for the poor.

The Lord gave the word:
  Great was the company of those that published it.
The chariots of God are twenty thousand, even thousands of angels;
  The Lord is among them, as in Sinai, in the holy place.
Thou hast ascended on high, thou hast led captivity captive:
Thou hast received gifts for men;
  Yea, for the rebellious also, that the Lord God might dwell among them.
Blessed be the Lord, who daily loadeth us with benefits.
  Even the God of our salvation.
He that is our God is the God of salvation:
  And unto God the Lord belong the issues from death.
Bless ye God in the congregations,
  Even the Lord, from the fountain of Israel.
Thy God hath commanded thy strength:
  Strengthen, O God, that which thou hast wrought for us.
Sing unto God, ye kingdoms of the earth;
  O sing praises unto the Lord;
To him that rideth upon the heavens of heavens, which were of old;
  Lo, he doth send out his voice, and that a mighty voice.
Ascribe ye strength unto God:
  His excellency is over Israel, and his strength is in the clouds.
O God, thou art terrible out of thy holy places:

The God of Israel is he that giveth strength and
  power unto his people.
    Blessed be God.

PSALM LXIX.

Save me, O God;
  For the waters are come in unto my soul.
I sink in deep mire, where there is no standing:
I am come into deep waters,
  Where the floods overflow me.
O God, thou knowest my foolishness;
  And my sins are not hid from thee.
But as for me, my prayer is unto thee, O Lord,
In an acceptable time: O God, in the multitude of
  thy mercy
    Hear me, in the truth of thy salvation.
Deliver me out of the mire, and let me not sink:
  Let me be delivered from them that hate me,
    and out of the deep waters.
Let not the water-flood overflow me,
Neither let the deep swallow me up,
  And let not the pit shut her mouth upon me.
Hear me, O Lord; for thy loving-kindness is good:
  Turn unto me according to the multitude of
    thy tender mercies.
And hide not thy face from thy servant;
  For I am in trouble: hear me speedily.
Draw nigh unto my soul, and redeem it:
  Deliver me because of mine enemies.
But I am poor and sorrowful:
  Let thy salvation, O God, set me up on high.
I will praise the name of God with a song,

And will magnify him with thanksgiving.
This also shall please the Lord better than an ox
    Or bullock that hath horns and hoofs.
The humble shall see this, and be glad:
    And your heart shall live that seek God.
For the Lord heareth the poor,
    And despiseth not his prisoners.
Let the heaven and earth praise him,
    The seas, and every thing that moveth therein.
For God will save Zion.
And will build the cities of Judah:
    That they may dwell there, and have it in possession.
The seed also of his servants shall inherit it:
    And they that love his name shall dwell therein.

PSALM LXXI.

In thee, O Lord, do I put my trust:
    Let me never be put to confusion.
Deliver me in thy righteousness, and cause me to escape:
    Incline thine ear unto me, and save me.
Be thou my strong habitation,
    Whereunto I may continually resort:
Thou hast given commandment to save me;
    For thou art my rock and my fortress.
Deliver me, O my God, out of the hand of the wicked,
    Out of the hand of the unrighteous and cruel man.
For thou art my hope,

O Lord God: thou art my trust from my
youth.
Let my mouth be filled with thy praise
And with thy honor all the day.
Cast me not off in the time of old age;
Forsake me not when my strength faileth.
But I will hope continually.
And will yet praise thee more and more.
My mouth shall show forth thy righteousness
And thy salvation all the day;
For I know not the numbers thereof.
I will go in the strength of the Lord God:
I will make mention of thy righteousness, even
of thine only.
O God, thou hast taught me from my youth:
And hitherto have I declared thy wondrous
works.
Now also when I am old and grayheaded, O God,
forsake me not;
Until I have showed thy strength unto this generation,
And thy power to every one that is to come.
Thy righteousness also, O God, is very high,
Who hast done great things.
O God, who is like unto thee!
Thou, which hast showed me great and sore troubles,
Shalt quicken me again,
And shalt bring me up again from the depths
of the earth.
Thou shalt increase my greatness,
And comfort me on every side.
I will also praise thee with the psaltery,
Even thy truth, O my God:

Unto thee will I sing with the harp, O thou
    Holy One of Israel.
My lips shall greatly rejoice when I sing unto thee;
    And my soul, which thou hast redeemed.
My tongue also shall talk of thy righteousness all
  the day long:
    For they are confounded, for they are brought
    unto shame, that seek my hurt.

PSALM LXXXII.

God standeth in the congregation of the mighty;
    He judgeth among the gods.
How long will ye judge unjustly,
    And accept the persons of the wicked?
Defend the poor and fatherless:
    Do justice to the afflicted and needy.
Deliver the poor and needy:
    Rid them out of the hand of the wicked.
They know not, neither will they understand;
They walk on in darkness:
    All the foundations of the earth are out of
    course.
I have said, Ye are gods;
    And all of you are children of the Most High.
But ye shall die like men,
    And fall like one of the princes.
Arise, O God, judge the earth:
    For thou shalt inherit all nations.

PSALM LXXXIV.

How amiable are thy tabernacles,
    O Lord of hosts!
My soul longeth, yea, even fainteth for the courts of the Lord:
    My heart and my flesh crieth out for the living God.
As the sparrow hath found an house, and the swallow a nest for herself,
    Where she may lay her young,
Even so am I at thine altars, O Lord of hosts,
    My King, and my God.
Blessed are they that dwell in thy house:
    They will be still praising thee.
Blessed is the man whose strength is in thee:
    In whose heart are thy ways.
Who passing through the desert valley of Baca make it a well;
    The rain also filleth the pools.
They go from strength to strength,
    Every one of them in Zion appeareth before God.
O Lord God of hosts, hear my prayer:
    Give ear, O God of Jacob.
Behold, O God our shield,
    And look upon the face of thine anointed.
For a day in thy courts is better than a thousand elsewhere.
I had rather be a doorkeeper in the house of my God,
    Than to dwell in the tents of wickedness.
For the Lord God is a sun and shield:

The Lord will give grace and glory:
> No good thing will he withhold from them that walk uprightly.

O Lord of hosts,
> Blessed is the man that trusteth in thee.

PSALM LXXXV.

Lord, thou hast been favorable unto thy land:
> Thou hast brought back the captivity of Jacob.

Thou hast forgiven the iniquity of thy people:
> Thou hast covered all their sin.

Thou hast taken away all thy wrath:
> Thou hast turned thyself from the fierceness of thine anger.

Turn us, O God of our salvation,
> And cause thine anger toward us to cease.

Wilt thou be angry with us for ever?
> Wilt thou draw out thine anger to all generations?

Wilt thou not revive us again:
> That thy people may rejoice in thee?

Show us thy mercy, O Lord,
> And grant us thy salvation.

I will hear what God the Lord will speak:
> For he will speak peace unto his people,

And to his saints:
> But let them not turn again to folly.

Surely his salvation is nigh them that fear him:
> That glory may dwell in our land.

Mercy and truth are met together;
> Righteousness and peace have kissed each other.

Truth shall spring out of the earth;

And righteousness shall look down from heaven.
Yea, the Lord shall give that which is good;
    And our land shall yield her increase.
Righteousness shall go before him;
    And shall set us in the way of his steps.

PSALM LXXXVI.

Bow down thine ear, O Lord, hear me:
    For I am poor and needy.
Preserve my soul; for thou art my hope:
O thou my God, save thy servant
    That trusteth in thee.
Be merciful unto me, O Lord:
    For I cry unto thee daily.
Rejoice the soul of thy servant:
    For unto thee, O Lord, do I lift up my soul.
For thou, Lord, art good, and ready to forgive;
    And plenteous in mercy unto all them that call
        upon thee.
Give ear, O Lord, unto my prayer;
    And attend to the voice of my supplications.
In the day of my trouble I will call upon thee:
    For thou wilt answer me.
Among the gods there is none like unto thee, O Lord;
    Neither are there any works like unto thy works.
All nations whom thou hast made
Shall come and worship before thee, O Lord;
    And shall glorify thy name.
For thou art great and doest wondrous things:
    Thou art God alone.
Teach me thy way, O Lord; I will walk in thy truth:
    Unite my heart to fear thy name.

I will praise thee, O Lord my God, with all my
  heart:
    And I will glorify thy name for evermore.
For great is thy mercy toward me:
    And thou hast delivered my soul from the ter-
      rors of death.
O God, the proud are risen against me,
And the assemblies of violent men have sought after
  my soul;
    And have not set thee before them.
But thou, O Lord, art a God full of compassion, and
  gracious,
    Long-suffering and plenteous in mercy and truth.
O turn unto me, and have mercy upon me;
Give thy strength unto thy servant,
    And save the son of thine handmaid.
Show me a token for good;
That they which hate me may see it, and be ashamed:
    Because thou, Lord, hast holpen me, and com-
      forted me.

PSALM LXXXIX.

I will sing of the mercies of the Lord for ever:
    With my mouth will I make known thy faith-
      fulness to all generations.
For I have said, Mercy shall be built up for ever:
    Thy faithfulness shalt thou establish in the very
      heavens.
And the heavens shall praise thy wonders, O Lord:
    Thy faithfulness also in the congregation of the
      saints.

For who in the heaven can be compared unto the
  Lord?
    Who among the sons of the mighty can be
      likened unto the Lord?
God is greatly to be feared in the assembly of the
  saints,
    And to be had in reverence of all them that
      are about him.
O Lord God of hosts,
Who is a strong Lord like unto thee?
    Or to thy faithfulness round about thee?
Thou rulest the raging of the sea:
    When the waves thereof arise, thou stillest them.
Thou hast broken Egypt in pieces, as one that is
  slain;
    Thou hast scattered thine enemies with thy
      strong arm.
The heavens are thine, the earth also is thine:
    As for the world and the fulness thereof, thou
      hast founded them.
The north and the south thou hast created them:
    Tabor and Hermon shall rejoice in thy name.
Thou hast a mighty arm:
    Strong is thy hand, and high is thy right hand.
Justice and judgment are the habitation of thy
  throne:
    Mercy and truth shall go before thy face.
Blessed is the people that know the joyful sound:
    They shall walk, O Lord, in the light of thy
      countenance.
In thy name shall they rejoice all the day:
    And in thy righteousness shall they be exalted.
For thou art the glory of their strength:

And in thy favor our horn shall be exalted.
For the Lord is our defence;
    And the Holy One of Israel is our king.

PSALM XC.

Lord, thou hast been our dwelling-place
    In all generations.
Before the mountains were brought forth,
Or ever thou hadst formed the earth and the world,
    Even from everlasting to everlasting, thou art God.
Thou turnest man to destruction;
    And sayest, Return, ye children of men.
For a thousand years in thy sight
Are but as yesterday when it is past,
    And as a watch in the night.
Thou carriest them away as with a flood; they are as a sleep:
    In the morning they are like grass which groweth up.
In the morning it flourisheth, and groweth up;
    In the evening it is cut down, and withereth.
For we are consumed by thine anger,
    And by thy wrath are we troubled.
Thou hast set our iniquities before thee,
    Our secret sins in the light of thy countenance.
For all our days are passed away in thy wrath:
    We spend our years as a tale that is told.
The days of our years are threescore years and ten;
    And if by reason of strength they be fourscore years,

Yet is their strength labor and sorrow;
    For it is soon cut off, and we fly away.
Who knoweth the power of thine anger?
    Even according to thy fear, so is thy wrath.
So teach us to number our days,
    That we may apply our hearts unto wisdom.
Return, O Lord, how long?
    And let it repent thee concerning thy servants.
O satisfy us early with thy mercy;
    That we may rejoice and be glad all our days.
Make us glad according to the days wherein thou hast afflicted us,
    And the years wherein we have seen evil.
Let thy work appear unto thy servants,
    And thy glory unto their children.
And let the beauty of the Lord our God be upon us:
And establish thou the work of our hands upon us;
    Yea, the work of our hands establish thou it.

PSALM XCI.

He that dwelleth in the secret place of the Most High
    Shall abide under the shadow of the Almighty.
I will say of the Lord, he is my refuge and my fortress:
    My God; in him will I trust.
Surely he shall deliver thee from the snare of the fowler,
    And from the noisome pestilence.
He shall cover thee with his feathers,
And under his wings shalt thou trust:
    His truth shall be thy shield and buckler.

Thou shalt not be afraid for the terror by night;
> Nor for the arrow that flieth by day;

Nor for the pestilence that walketh in darkness;
> Nor for the destruction that wasteth at noonday.

A thousand shall fall at thy side,
And ten thousand at thy right hand;
> But it shall not come nigh thee.

Only with thine eyes shalt thou behold
> And see the reward of the wicked.

Because thou hast made the Lord, which is my refuge,
> Even the Most High, thy habitation;

There shall no evil befall thee,
> Neither shall any plague come nigh thy dwelling.

For he shall give his angels charge over thee,
> To keep thee in all thy ways.

They shall bear thee up in their hands,
> Lest thou dash thy foot against a stone.

Thou shalt tread upon the lion and adder:
> The young lion and the dragon shalt thou trample under feet.

Because he hath set his love upon me, therefore will I deliver him:
> I will set him on high, because he hath known my name.

He shall call upon me, and I will answer him:
I will be with him in trouble;
> I will deliver him, and honor him.

With long life will I satisfy him,
> And show him my salvation.

PSALM XCIII.

The Lord reigneth, he is clothed with majesty;
The Lord is clothed with strength, wherewith he
   hath girded himself:
      The world also is stablished, that it cannot be
         moved.
Thy throne is established of old;
      Thou art from everlasting.
The floods have lifted up, O Lord,
The floods have lifted up their voice;
      The floods lift up their waves.
The Lord on high is mightier than the noise of many
   waters,
      Yea, than the mighty waves of the sea.
Thy testimonies are very sure:
Holiness becometh thine house,
      O Lord, for ever.

PSALM XCVII.

The Lord reigneth; let the earth rejoice;
   Let the multitude of isles be glad thereof.
Clouds and darkness are round about him:
      Righteousness and judgment are the habitation
         of his throne.
A fire goeth before him,
   And burneth up his enemies round about.
His lightnings enlightened the world:
      The earth saw, and trembled.
The hills melted like wax at the presence of the
   Lord,

At the presence of the Lord of the whole earth.
The heavens declare his righteousness,
　　And all the people see his glory.
Confounded be all they that serve graven images,
That boast themselves of idols:
　　Worship him, all ye gods.
Zion heard, and was glad;
And the daughters of Judah rejoiced
　　Because of thy judgments, O Lord.
For thou, Lord, art high above all the earth:
　　Thou art exalted far above all gods.
Ye that love the Lord, hate evil:
He preserveth the souls of his saints;
　　He delivereth them out of the hand of the wicked.
Light is shown for the righteous,
　　And gladness for the upright in heart.
Rejoice in the Lord, ye righteous;
　　And give thanks at the remembrance of his holiness.

PSALM CII.

HEAR my prayer, O Lord,
　　And let my cry come unto thee.
Hide not thy face from me, in the day when I am in trouble;
Incline thine ear unto me:
　　In the day when I call, answer me speedily.
For my days are consumed like smoke,
　　And my bones are burned as a firebrand.
I am like a pelican of the wilderness:
　　I am like an owl of the desert.

I watch, and am as a sparrow
  Alone upon the house-top.
Mine enemies reproach me all the day;
  And they that are mad against me are sworn
    against me.
For I have eaten ashes like bread,
  And mingled my drink with weeping,
Because of thine indignation and thy wrath:
  For thou hast lifted me up, and cast me down.
My days are like a shadow that declineth;
  And I am withered like grass.
But thou, O Lord, shalt endure for ever;
  And thy remembrance unto all generations.
Thou shalt arise, and have mercy upon Zion:
  For the time to favor her, yea, the set time, is
    come.
For thy servants take pleasure in her stones,
  And favor the dust thereof.
So the heathen shall fear the name of the Lord,
  And all the kings of the earth thy glory.
When the Lord shall build up Zion,
  He shall appear in his glory.
He will regard the prayer of the destitute,
  And not despise their prayer.
This shall be written for the generations to come:
  And the people which shall be created shall
    praise the Lord.
For he hath looked down from the height of his
  sanctuary;
  From heaven did the Lord behold the earth;
To hear the groaning of the prisoner;
  To loose those that are appointed to death;
To declare the name of the Lord in Zion,

And his praise in Jerusalem;
When the people are gathered together,
And the kingdoms, to serve the Lord.
I said, O my God, take me not away in the midst of
my days:
Thy years are throughout all generations.
Of old hast thou laid the foundation of the earth:
And the heavens are the work of thy hands.
They shalt perish, but thou shalt endure:
Yea, all of them shall wax old like a garment;
As a vesture shalt thou change them, and they
shall be changed:
But thou art the same,
And thy years shall have no end.
The children of thy servants shall continue,
And their seed shall be established before thee.

PSALM CIII.

Bless the Lord, O my soul:
And all that is within me, bless his holy name.
Bless the Lord, O my soul,
And forget not all his benefits:
Who forgiveth all thine iniquities;
Who healeth all thy diseases;
Who redeemeth thy life from destruction;
Who crowneth thee with loving-kindness and
tender mercies;
Who satisfieth thy mouth with good things;
So that thy youth is renewed like the eagle's.
The Lord executeth righteousness
And judgment for all that are oppressed.
He made known his ways unto Moses,

His acts unto the children of Israel.
The Lord is merciful and gracious,
　　Slow to anger, and plenteous in mercy
He will not always chide:
　　Neither will he keep his anger for ever.
He hath not dealt with us after our sins;
　　Nor rewarded us according to our iniquities.
For as the heaven is high above the earth,
　　So great is his mercy toward them that fear him.
As far as the east is from the west,
　　So far hath he removed our transgressions from us.
Like as a father pitieth his children.
　　So the Lord pitieth them that fear him.
For he knoweth our frame;
　　He remembereth that we are dust.
As for man, his days are as grass:
　　As a flower of the field, so he flourisheth.
For the wind passeth over it, and it is gone;
　　And the place thereof shall know it no more.
But the mercy of the Lord is from everlasting to everlasting upon them that fear him,
　　And his righteousness unto children's children;
To such as keep his covenant,
　　And to those that remember his commandments to do them.
The Lord hath prepared his throne in the heavens;
　　And his kingdom ruleth over all.
Bless the Lord, ye his angels,
That excel in strength, that do his commandments,
　　Hearken unto the voice of his word.
Bless ye the Lord, all ye his hosts;

Ye ministers of his, that do his pleasure.
Bless the Lord, all his works
In all places of his dominion:
    Bless the Lord, O my soul.

PSALM CIV.

Bless the Lord, O my soul.
O Lord my God, thou art very great;
    Thou art clothed with honor and majesty.
Who coverest thyself with light as with a garment:
    Who stretchest out the heavens like a curtain:
Who layeth the beams of his chambers in the waters:
Who maketh the clouds his chariot:
    Who walketh upon the wings of the wind:
Who maketh his angels spirits;
    His ministers a flaming fire:
Who laid the foundations of the earth,
    That it should not be removed for ever.
Thou coveredst it with the deep as with a garment:
    The waters stood above the mountains.
At thy rebuke they fled;
    At the voice of thy thunder they hasted away.
They go up by the mountains; they go down by the valleys
    Unto the place which thou hast founded for them.
Thou hast set a bound that they may not pass over;
    That they turn not again to cover the earth.
He sendeth the springs into the valleys,
    Which run among the hills.
They give drink to every beast of the field:
    The wild asses quench their thirst.

By them shall the fowls of the heaven have their habitation,
    Which sing among the branches.
He watereth the hills from his chambers:
    The earth is satisfied with the fruit of thy works.
He causeth the grass to grow for the cattle,
    And herb for the service of man:
That he may bring forth food out of the earth;
    And wine that maketh glad the heart of man,
And oil to make his face to shine,
    And bread which strengtheneth man's heart.
The trees of the Lord are full of sap;
    The cedars of Lebanon, which he hath planted;
Where the birds make their nests:
    As for the stork, the fir-trees are her house.
The high hills are a refuge for the wild goats;
    And the rocks for the conies.
He appointed the moon for seasons:
    The sun knoweth his going down.
Thou makest darkness, and it is night:
    Wherein all the beasts of the forest do creep forth.
The young lions roar after their prey,
    And seek their meat from God.
The sun ariseth, they gather themselves together,
    And lay them down in their dens.
Man goeth forth unto his work,
    And to his labor, until the evening.
O Lord, how manifold are thy works!
    In wisdom hast thou made them all:
The earth is full of thy riches.
    So is this great and wide sea,
Wherein are things creeping innumerable,

Both small and great beasts.
There go the ships:
  There is that leviathan, whom thou hast made to play therein.
These wait all upon thee;
  That thou mayest give them their meat in due season.
That thou givest them, they gather:
  Thou openest thine hand, they are filled with good.
Thou hidest thy face, they are troubled:
Thou takest away their breath, they die,
  And return to their dust.
Thou sendest forth thy spirit, they are created:
  And thou renewest the face of the earth.
The glory of the Lord shall endure for ever:
  The Lord shall rejoice in his works.
He looketh on the earth, and it trembleth:
  He toucheth the hills, and they smoke.
I will sing unto the Lord as long as I live:
  I will sing praise to my God while I have my being.
My meditation of him shall be sweet:
  I will be glad in the Lord.
Let the sinners be consumed out of the earth,
  And let the wicked be no more.
Bless thou the Lord, O my soul.
  Praise ye the Lord.

PSALM CVII.

O give thanks unto the Lord, for he is good:
  For his mercy endureth forever.

Let the redeemed of the Lord say so,
>Whom he hath redeemed from the hand of the enemy;

And gathered them out of the lands,
>From the east, and from the west, from the north, and from the south.

They wandered in the wilderness in a solitary way;
>They found no city to dwell in.

Hungry and thirsty,
>Their soul fainted in them.

Then they cried unto the Lord in their trouble,
>And he delivered them out of their distresses

And he led them forth by the right way,
>That they might go to a city of habitation.

Oh that men would praise the Lord for his goodness,
>And for his wonderful works to the children of men!

For he satisfieth the longing soul,
>And filleth the hungry soul with goodness.

Such as sit in darkness and in the shadow of death,
>Being bound in affliction and iron;

Because they rebelled against the words of God,
>And contemned the counsel of the Most High:

Therefore he brought down their heart with labor:
>They fell down, and there was none to help.

Then they cried unto the Lord in their trouble,
>And he saved them out of their distresses.

He brought them out of darkness and the shadow of death,
>And brake their bands in sunder.

Oh that men would praise the Lord for his goodness.
>And for his wonderful works to the children of men!

For he hath broken the gates of brass,
> And cut the bars of iron in sunder.

Fools, because of their transgression,
> And because of their iniquities, are afflicted.

Their soul abhorreth all manner of meat;
> And they draw near unto the gates of death.

Then they cry unto the Lord in their trouble,
> And he saveth them out of their distresses.

He sent his word, and healed them,
> And delivered them from their destructions.

Oh that men would praise the Lord for his goodness.
> And for his wonderful works to the children of men!

And let them sacrifice the sacrifices of thanksgiving,
> And declare his works with rejoicing.

They that go down to the sea in ships,
> That do business in great waters;

These see the works of the Lord,
> And his wonders in the deep.

For he commandeth and raiseth the stormy wind,
> Which lifteth up the waves thereof.

They mount up to the heaven, they go down again to the depths:
> Their soul is melted because of trouble.

They reel to and fro, and stagger like a drunken man,
> And are at their wit's end.

Then they cry unto the Lord in their trouble,
> And he bringeth them out of their distresses.

He maketh the storm a calm,
> So that the waves thereof are still.

Then are they glad because they be quiet;
> So he bringeth them unto their desired haven.

Oh that men would praise the Lord for his goodness.

And for his wonderful works to the children of men!
Let them exalt him also in the congregation of the people,
And praise him in the assembly of the elders.
He turneth rivers into a wilderness,
And the water-springs into dry ground;
A fruitful land into barrenness,
For the wickedness of them that dwell therein.
He turneth the wilderness into a standing water,
And dry ground into water-springs.
And there he maketh the hungry to dwell,
That they may prepare a city for habitation;
And sow the fields, and plant vineyards,
Which may yield fruits of increase.
He blesseth them also, so that they are multiplied greatly;
And suffereth not their cattle to decrease.
Again, they are minished and brought low
Through oppression, affliction, and sorrow.
He poureth contempt upon princes,
And causeth them to wander in the wilderness, where there is no way.
Yet setteth he the poor on high from affliction,
And maketh him families like a flock.
The righteous shall see it, and rejoice:
And all iniquity shall stop her mouth.
Whoso is wise, and will observe these things,
Even they shall understand the loving-kindness of the Lord.

PSALM CX.

The Lord said unto my Lord, Sit thou at my right hand,
    Until I make thine enemies thy footstool.
The Lord shall send the sceptre of thy strength out of Zion;
    Rule thou in the midst of thine enemies.
Thy people shall give willingly in the day of thy power, in the beauties of holiness.
    From the womb of the morning thou hast the dew of thy youth.
The Lord hath sworn, and will not repent,
Thou art a priest for ever
    After the order of Melchizedek.
The Lord at thy right hand
    Shall strike through kings in the day of his wrath.
He shall judge among the heathen, he shall fill the places with the dead bodies;
    He shall wound the heads of his enemies over great countries.
Thou shalt drink of the brook in the way:
    Therefore shalt thou lift up the head.

PSALM CXI.

Praise ye the Lord.
I will praise the Lord with my whole heart,
    In the assembly of the upright, and in the congregation.
The works of the Lord are great,

Sought out of all them that have pleasure
    therein.
His work is honorable and glorious:
    And his righteousness endureth for ever.
He hath made his wonderful works to be remembered:
    The Lord is gracious and full of compassion.
He hath given meat unto them that fear him:
    He will ever be mindful of his covenant.
He hath showed his people the power of his works,
    That he may give them the heritage of the
    heathen.
The works of his hands are verity and judgment;
    All his commandments are sure:
They stand fast for ever and ever,
    And are done in truth and uprightness.
He sent redemption unto his people:
He hath commanded his covenant for ever:
    Holy and reverend is his name.
The fear of the Lord is the beginning of wisdom:
A good understanding have all they that do his
commandments.
    His praise endureth for ever.

PSALM CXII.

PRAISE ye the Lord.
Blessed is the man that feareth the Lord,
    That delighteth greatly in his commandments.
His seed shall be mighty upon earth:
    The generation of the upright shall be blessed.
Wealth and riches shall be in his house:
    And his righteousness endureth for ever.

Unto the upright there ariseth light in the darkness:
> He is gracious, and full of compassion, and righteous.

A good man showeth favor, and lendeth:
> He will guide his affairs with discretion.

Surely he shall not be moved for ever:
> The righteous shall be in everlasting remembrance.

He shall not be afraid of evil tidings:
> His heart is fixed, trusting in the Lord.

His heart is established, he shall not be afraid,
> Until he see his desire upon his enemies.

He hath scattered, he hath given to the poor;
His righteousness endureth for ever;
> His horn shall be exalted with honor.

The wicked shall see it, and be grieved;
He shall gnash with his teeth, and melt away:
> The desire of the wicked shall perish.

PSALM CXIII.

Praise ye the Lord.
Praise, O ye servants of the Lord,
> Praise the name of the Lord,

Blessed be the name of the Lord
> From this time forth and for evermore.

From the rising of the sun unto the going down of the same
> The Lord's name is to be praised.

The Lord is high above all nations,
> And his glory above the heavens.

Who is like unto the Lord our God,
> Who dwelleth on high,

Who humbleth himself to behold
  The things that are in heaven, and in the earth!
He raiseth up the poor out of the dust,
  And lifteth the needy out of the dunghill;
That he may set him with princes,
  Even with the princes of his people.
He maketh the barren woman to keep house,
And to be a joyful mother of children.
  Praise ye the Lord.

PSALM CXIV.

When Israel went out of Egypt,
  The house of Jacob from a people of strange language;
Judah was his sanctuary,
  And Israel his dominion.
The sea saw it, and fled:
  Jordan was driven back.
The mountains skipped like rams,
  And the little hills like lambs.
What ailed thee, O thou sea, that thou fleddest?
  Thou Jordan, that thou wast driven back?
Ye mountains, that ye skipped like rams;
  And ye little hills, like lambs?
Tremble thou earth, at the presence of the Lord,
  At the presence of the God of Jacob;
Which turned the rock into a standing water,
  The flint into a fountain of waters.

PSALM CXV.

Not unto us, O Lord, not unto us,
But unto thy name give glory,
   For thy mercy, and for thy truth's sake.
Wherefore should the heathen say,
   Where is now their God?
But our God is in the heavens:
   He hath done whatsoever he hath pleased.
Their idols are silver and gold,
   The work of men's hands.
They have mouths, but they speak not:
   Eyes have they, but they see not:
They have ears, but they hear not:
   Noses have they, but they smell not:
They have hands, but they handle not:
Feet have they, but they walk not:
   Neither speak they through their throat.
They that make them are like unto them;
   So is every one that trusteth in them.
O Israel, trust thou in the Lord:
   He is their help and their shield.
O house of Aaron trust in the Lord:
   He is their help and their shield.
Ye that fear the Lord, trust in the Lord:
   He is their help and their shield.
The Lord hath been mindful of us: he will bless us;
   He will bless the house of Israel;
   He will bless the house of Aaron.
He will bless them that fear the Lord,
   Both small and great.
The Lord shall increase you more and more,
   You and your children.

Ye are blessed of the Lord
> Which made heaven and earth.

The heaven, even the heavens, are the Lord's:
> But the earth hath he given to the children of men.

The dead praise not the Lord,
> Neither any that go down into silence.

But we will bless the Lord
From this time forth and for evermore.
> Praise the Lord.

PSALM CXVI.

I love the Lord, because he hath heard
> My voice and my supplications.

Because he hath inclined his ear unto me.
> Therefore will I call upon him as long as I live

The sorrows of death compassed me,
And the pains of hell gat hold upon me:
> I found trouble and sorrow.

Then called I upon the name of the Lord;
> O Lord, I beseech thee, deliver my soul.

Gracious is the Lord, and righteous;
> Yea, our God is merciful.

The Lord preserveth the simple:
> I was brought low, and he helped me.

Return unto thy rest, O my soul;
> For the Lord hath dealt bountifully with thee.

For thou hast delivered my soul from death,
Mine eyes from tears,
> And my feet from falling.

I will walk before the Lord
> In the land of the living.

I believed, therefore have I spoken:
> I was greatly afflicted:
I said in my haste,
> All men are liars.
What shall I render unto the Lord
> For all his benefits towards me?
I will take the cup of salvation,
> And call upon the name of the Lord.
I will pay my vows unto the Lord
> Now in the presence of all his people.
Precious in the sight of the Lord
> Is the death of his saints.
O Lord, truly I am thy servant;
I am thy servant, and the son of thine handmaid:
> Thou hast loosed my bonds.
I will offer to thee the sacrifice of thanksgiving,
> And will call upon the name of the Lord.
I will pay my vows unto the Lord
> Now in the presence of all his people.
In the courts of the Lord's house,
In the midst of thee, O Jerusalem.
> Praise ye the Lord.

PSALM CXVII.

O praise the Lord, all ye nations:
> Praise him, all ye people.
For his merciful kindness is great towards us:
> And the truth of the Lord endureth for ever.
Praise ye the Lord.

PSALM CXVIII.

O GIVE thanks unto the Lord; for he is good:
    Because his mercy endureth for ever.
Let Israel now say,
    That his mercy endureth for ever.
Let the house of Aaron now say,
    That his mercy endureth for ever.
Let them now that fear the Lord say,
    That his mercy endureth for ever.
I called upon the Lord in distress:
    The Lord answered me, and set me in a large place.
The Lord is on my side; I will not fear:
    What can man do unto me?
The Lord taketh my part with them that help me:
    Therefore shall I see my desire upon them that hate me.
It is better to trust in the Lord
    Than to put confidence in man.
It is better to trust in the Lord
    Than to put confidence in princes.
The Lord is my strength and song,
    And is become my salvation.
The voice of rejoicing and salvation
Is in the tabernacles of the righteous:
    The right hand of the Lord doeth valiantly.
The right hand of the Lord is exalted:
    The right hand of the Lord doeth valiantly.
I shall not die, but live,
    And declare the works of the Lord.
The Lord hath chastened me sore:
    But he hath not given me over unto death.

Open to me the gates of righteousness:
    I will go into them, and I will praise the Lord:
This gate of the Lord,
    Into which the righteous shall enter.
I will praise thee: for thou hast heard me,
    And art become my salvation.
The stone which the builders refused
    Is become the head-stone of the corner.
This is the Lord's doing;
    It is marvellous in our eyes.
This is the day which the Lord hath made;
    We will rejoice and be glad in it.
Save now, I beseech thee, O Lord:
    O Lord, I beseech thee, send now prosperity.
Blessed be he that cometh in the name of the Lord:
    We have blessed you out of the house of the Lord.
Thou art my God, and I will praise thee:
    Thou art my God, I will exalt thee.
O give thanks unto the Lord; for he is good:
    For his mercy endureth for ever

PSALM CXIX.

Blessed are the undefiled in the way,
    Who walketh in the law of the Lord.
Blessed are they that keep his testimonies,
    And that seek him with the whole heart.
They also do no iniquity:
    They walk in his ways.
Thou hast commanded us
    To keep thy precepts diligently.
O that my ways were directed

To keep thy statutes!
Then shall I not be ashamed,
  When I have respect unto all thy command-
    ments.
I will praise thee with uprightness of heart,
  When I shall have learned thy righteous judg-
    ments.
I will keep thy statutes:
  O forsake me not utterly.

Wherewithal shall a young man cleanse his way?
  By taking heed thereto according to thy word.
With my whole heart have I sought thee:
  O let me not wander from thy commandments.
Thy word have I hid in mine heart,
  That I might not sin against thee.
Blessed art thou, O Lord:
  Teach me thy statutes.
With my lips have I declared
  All the judgments of thy mouth.
I have rejoiced in the way of thy testimonies,
  As much as in all riches.
I will meditate in thy precepts,
  And have respect unto thy ways.
I will delight myself in thy statutes:
  I will not forget thy word.

My soul cleaveth unto the dust:
  Quicken thou me according to thy word.
I have declared my ways, and thou heardest me;
  Teach me thy statutes.
Make me to understand the way of thy precepts:
  So shall I talk of thy wondrous works.

My soul melteth for heaviness:
> Strengthen thou me according unto thy word.

Remove from me the way of lying:
> And grant me thy law graciously.

'ave chosen the way of truth:
> Thy judgments have I laid before me.

I have stuck unto thy testimonies:
> O Lord, put me not to shame.

I will run the way of thy commandments,
> When thou shalt enlarge my heart.

Teach me, O Lord, the way of thy statutes;
> And I shall keep it unto the end.

Give me understanding, and I shall keep thy law;
> Yea, I shall observe it with my whole heart.

Make me to go in the path of thy commandments;
> For therein do I delight.

Incline my heart unto thy testimonies,
> And not to covetousness.

Turn away mine eyes from beholding vanity;
> And quicken thou me in thy way.

Stablish thy word unto thy servant,
> Who is devoted to thy fear.

Turn away my reproach which I fear:
> For thy judgments are good.

Behold, I have longed after thy precepts:
> Quicken me in thy righteousness.

Let thy mercies come also unto me, O Lord,
> Even thy salvation, according to thy word.

So shall I have wherewith to answer him that reproacheth me:

> For I trust in thy word.
And take not the word of truth utterly out of my mouth;
> For I have hoped in thy judgments.
So shall I keep thy law continually
> For ever and ever.
And I will walk at liberty:
> For I seek thy precepts.
I will speak of thy testimonies also before kings.
> And will not be ashamed.
And I will delight myself in thy commandments,
> Which I have loved.
My hands also will I lift up unto thy commandments, which I have loved;
> And I will meditate in thy statutes.

Thy hands have made me and fashioned me:
> Give me understanding, that I may learn thy commandments.
They that fear thee will be glad when they see me;
> Because I have hoped in thy word.
I know, O Lord, that thy judgments are right,
> And that thou in faithfulness hast afflicted me.
Let, I pray thee, thy merciful kindness be for my comfort,
> According to thy word unto thy servant.
Let thy tender mercies come unto me, that I may live:
> For thy law is my delight.
Let the proud be ashamed; for they dealt perversely with me without a cause:
> But I will meditate in thy precepts.
Let those that fear thee turn unto me,

And those that have known thy testimonies.
Let my heart be sound in thy statutes:
    That I be not ashamed.

My soul fainteth for thy salvation:
    But I hope in thy word.
Mine eyes fail for thy word,
    Saying, When wilt thou comfort me?
For I am become like a bottle in the smoke;
    Yet do I not forget thy statutes.
How many are the days of thy servant?
    When wilt thou execute judgment on them that persecute me?
The proud have digged pits for me,
    Which are not after thy law.
All thy commandments are faithful:
    They persecute me wrongfully; help thou me.
They had almost consumed me upon earth;
    But I forsook not thy precepts.
Quicken me after thy loving-kindness;
    So shall I keep the testimony of thy mouth.

For ever, O Lord,
    Thy word is settled in heaven.
Thy faithfulness is unto all generations:
    Thou hast established the earth, and it abideth.
They continue this day according to thine ordinances:
    For all are thy servants.
Unless thy law had been my delights,
    I should then have perished in mine affliction.
I will never forget thy precepts:
    For with them thou hast quickened me.
I am thine save me;

For I have sought thy precepts.
The wicked have waited for me to destroy me:
But I will consider thy testimonies.
I have seen an end of all perfection:
But thy commandment is exceeding broad.

O how love I thy law!
It is my meditation all the day.
Thou through thy commandments hast made me wiser than mine enemies:
For they are ever with me.
I have more understanding than all my teachers:
For thy testimonies are my meditation.
I understand more than the ancients,
Because I keep thy precepts.
I have refrained my feet from every evil way,
That I might keep thy word.
I have not departed from thy judgments:
For thou hast taught me.
How sweet are thy words unto my taste!
Yea, sweeter than honey to my mouth.
Through thy precepts I get understanding:
Therefore I hate every false way.

Thy testimonies are wonderful:
Therefore doth my soul keep them.
The entrance of thy words giveth light;
It giveth understanding unto the simple.
I opened my mouth, and panted;
For I longed for thy commandments.
Look thou upon me, and be merciful unto me,
As thou usest to do unto those that love thy name.

Order my steps in thy word:
    And let not any iniquity have dominion over me.
Deliver me from the oppression of man:
    So will I keep thy precepts.
Make thy face to shine upon thy servant;
    And teach me thy statutes.
Rivers of waters run down mine eyes,
    Because they keep not thy law.

Righteous art thou, O Lord,
    And upright are thy judgments.
Thy testimonies that thou hast commanded
    Are righteous and very faithful.
My zeal hath consumed me,
    Because mine enemies have forgotten thy words.
Thy word is very pure:
    Therefore thy servant loveth it.
I am small and despised:
    Yet do not I forget thy precepts.
Thy righteousness is an everlasting righteousness,
    And thy law is the truth.
Trouble and anguish have taken hold on me:
    Yet thy commandments are my delights.
The righteousness of thy testimonies is everlasting:
    Give me understanding, and I shall live.

I cried with my whole heart; Hear me, O Lord:
    I will keep thy statutes.
I cried unto thee; save me,
    And I shall keep thy testimonies.
I prevented the dawning of the morning, and cried:
    I hoped in thy word.
Mine eyes prevent the night watches,

That I might meditate in thy word.
Hear my voice according unto thy loving-kindness:
O Lord, quicken me according to thy judgment.
They draw nigh that follow after mischief:
They are far from thy law.
Thou art near, O Lord;
And all thy commandments are truth.
Concerning thy testimonies, I have known of old
That thou hast founded them for ever.

Let my cry come near before thee, O Lord:
Give me understanding according to thy word.
Let my supplication come before thee:
Deliver me according to thy word.
My lips shall utter praise,
When thou hast taught me thy statutes:
My tongue shall speak of thy word:
For all thy commandments are righteousness.
Let thine hand help me;
For I have chosen thy precepts.
I have longed for thy salvation, O Lord;
And thy law is my delight.
Let my soul live, and it shall praise thee;
And let thy judgments help me.
I have gone astray like a lost sheep:
Seek thy servant; for I do not forget thy commandments.

PSALM CXXIII.

Unto thee lift I up mine eyes,
O thou that dwellest in the heavens.
Behold, as the eyes of servants look unto the hand of their masters,

And as the eyes of a maiden unto the hand of
    her mistress;
So our eyes wait upon the Lord our God,
    Until that he have mercy upon us.
Have mercy upon us, O Lord, have mercy upon us;
    For we are exceedingly filled with contempt.
Our soul is exceedingly filled
With the scorning of those that are at ease,
    And with the contempt of the proud.

PSALM CXXX.

Out of the depths have I cried unto thee, O Lord.
    Lord, hear my voice:
Let thine ears be attentive
    To the voice of my supplications.
If thou, Lord, shouldest mark iniquities,
    O Lord, who shall stand?
But there is forgiveness with thee, that thou mayest
    be feared.
I wait for the Lord, my soul doth wait,
    And in his word do I hope.
My soul waiteth for the Lord
More than they that watch for the morning.
    I say, more than they that watch for the morning.
Let Israel hope in the Lord:
For with the Lord there is mercy,
    And with him is plenteous redemption.
And he shall redeem Israel
    From all his iniquities.

PSALM CXXXV.

Praise ye the Lord.
Praise ye the name of the Lord;
    Praise him, O ye servants of the Lord.
Ye that stand in the house of the Lord,
    In the courts of the house of our God,
Praise the Lord; for the Lord is good:
    Sing praises unto his name: for it is pleasant.
For the Lord hath chosen Jacob unto himself,
    And Israel for his peculiar treasure.
For I know that the Lord is great,
    And that our Lord is above all gods.
Whatsoever the Lord pleased, that did he,
    In heaven, and in earth, in the seas, and in all deep places.
He causeth the vapors to ascend from the ends of the earth;
He maketh lightnings for the rain;
    He bringeth the wind out of his treasuries.
Thy name, O Lord, endureth for ever;
    And thy memorial, O Lord, throughout all generations.
For the Lord will judge his people,
    And he will repent himself concerning his servants.
The idols of the heathen are silver and gold,
    The work of men's hands.
They have mouths, but they speak not;
    Eyes have they, but they see not;
They have ears, but they hear not;
    Neither is there any breath in their mouths.
They that make them are like unto them;

So is every one that trusteth in them.
Bless the Lord, O house of Israel:
Bless the Lord, O house of Aaron:
Bless the Lord, O house of Levi:
Ye that fear the Lord, bless the Lord.
Blessed be the Lord out of Zion, which dwelleth at Jerusalem.
Praise ye the Lord.

PSALM CXXXVI.

O GIVE thanks unto the Lord; for he is good:
For his mercy endureth for ever.
O give thanks unto the God of gods:
For his mercy endureth for ever.
O give thanks to the Lord of lords:
For his mercy endureth for ever.
To him who alone doeth great wonders:
For his mercy endureth for ever.
To him that by wisdom made the heavens:
For his mercy endureth for ever.
To him that stretched out the earth above the waters:
For his mercy endureth for ever.
To him that made great lights:
For his mercy endureth for ever.
The sun to rule by day:
For his mercy endureth for ever.
The moon and stars to rule by night:
For his mercy endureth for ever.
Who remembered us in our low estate:
For his mercy endureth for ever
And hath redeemed us from our enemies:

> For his mercy endureth for ever.
Who giveth food to all flesh:
> For his mercy endureth for ever.
O give thanks unto the God of heaven:
> For his mercy endureth for ever.

PSALM CXXXVIII.

I will praise thee with my whole heart:
> Before the gods will I sing praise unto thee.

I will worship toward thy holy temple,
And praise thy name, for thy loving-kindness and for thy truth:
> For thou hast magnified thy word above all thy name.

In the day when I cried thou answeredst me,
> And strengthenedst me with strength in my soul.

All the kings of the earth shall praise thee, O Lord,
> When they hear the words of thy mouth.

Yea, they shall sing in the ways of the Lord:
> For great is the glory of the Lord.

Though the Lord be high, yet hath he respect unto the lowly:
> But the proud he knoweth afar off.

Though I walk in the midst of trouble, thou wilt revive me:
Thou shalt stretch forth thine hand against the wrath of mine enemies,
> And thy right hand shall save me.

The Lord will perfect that which concerneth me:
Thy mercy, O Lord, endureth for ever:
> Forsake not the works of thine own hands.

PSALM CXXXIX.

O Lord, thou hast searched me, and known me.
Thou knowest my down-sitting and mine uprising,
    Thou understandest my thought afar off.
Thou compassest my path and my lying down,
    And art acquainted with all my ways.
For there is not a word in my tongue,
    But, lo, O Lord, thou knowest it altogether.
Thou hast beset me behind and before,
    And laid thine hand upon me.
Such knowledge is too wonderful for me;
    It is high, I cannot attain unto it.
Whither shall I go from thy spirit?
    Or whither shall I flee from thy presence?
If I ascend up into heaven, thou art there:
    If I make my bed in hell, behold thou art there.
If I take the wings of the morning,
    And dwell in the uttermost parts of the sea;
Even there shall thy hand lead me,
    And thy right hand shall hold me.
If I say, Surely the darkness shall cover me;
    Even the night shall be light about me.
Yea, the darkness hideth not from thee;
But the night shineth as the day:
    The darkness and the light are both alike to thee.
I will praise thee; for I am fearfully and wonderfully made:
Marvellous are thy works;
    And that my soul knoweth right well.
My substance was not hid from thee,

When I was made in secret,
>   And curiously wrought in the lowest parts of the earth.

Thine eyes did see my substance, yet being unperfect;
And in thy book all my members were written,
>   Which day by day were fashioned, when as yet there was none of them.

How precious also are thy thoughts unto me, O God!
>   How great is the sum of them!

If I should count them, they are more in number than the sand:
>   When I awake, I am still with thee.

Search me, O God, and know my heart:
>   Try me, and know my thoughts:

And see if there be any wicked way in me,
>   And lead me in the way everlasting.

PSALM CXLIII.

Hear my prayer, O Lord,
Give ear to my supplications:
>   In thy faithfulness answer me, and in thy righteousness.

And enter not into judgment with thy servant:
>   For in thy sight shall no man living be justified.

I remember the days of old;
I meditate on all thy works;
>   I muse on the work of thy hands.

I stretch forth my hands unto thee:
>   My soul thirsteth after thee, as a thirsty land.

Hear me speedily, O Lord; my spirit faileth:
Hide not thy face from me,

Lest I be like unto them that go down into the
   pit.
Cause me to hear thy loving-kindness in the morning;
   For in thee do I trust:
Cause me to know the way wherein I should walk;
   For I lift up my soul unto thee.
Deliver me, O Lord, from mine enemies:
   I flee unto thee to hide me.
Teach me to do thy will;
For thou art my God:
   Thy spirit is good; lead me into the land of
   uprightness.
Quicken me, O Lord, for thy name's sake:
   For thy righteousness' sake bring my soul out
   of trouble.

PSALM CXLV.

I will extol thee, my God, O King:
   And I will bless thy name for ever and ever.
Every day will I bless thee;
   And I will praise thy name for ever and ever.
Great is the Lord, and greatly to be praised;
   And his greatness is unsearchable.
One generation shall praise thy works to another,
   And shall declare thy mighty acts.
I will speak of the glorious honor of thy majesty,
   And of thy wondrous works.
And men shall speak of the might of thy terrible
   acts:
   And I will declare thy greatness.
They shall abundantly utter the memory of thy
   great goodness,

And shall sing of thy righteousness.
The Lord is gracious, and full of compassion;
　　Slow to anger, and of great mercy.
The Lord is good to all:
　　And his tender mercies are over all his works
All thy works shall praise thee, O Lord:
　　And thy saints shall bless thee.
They shall speak of the glory of thy kingdom,
　　And talk of thy power;
To make known to the sons of men his mighty acts,
　　And the glorious majesty of his kingdom.
Thy kingdom is an everlasting kingdom,
　　And thy dominion endureth throughout all generations.
The Lord upholdeth all that fall,
　　And raiseth up all those that be bowed down.
The eyes of all wait upon thee;
　　And thou givest them their meat in due season.
Thou openest thine hand,
　　And satisfiest the desire of every living thing.
The Lord is righteous in all his ways,
　　And holy in all his works.
The Lord is nigh unto all them that call upon him,
　　To all that call upon him in truth.
He will fulfil the desire of them that fear him:
　　He also will hear their cry, and will save them.
The Lord preserveth all them that love him:
　　But all the wicked will he destroy.
My mouth shall speak the praise of the Lord.
　　And let all flesh bless his holy name. For ever and ever.

PSALM CXLVI.

Praise ye the Lord.
    Praise the Lord, O my soul.
While I live I will praise the Lord:
    I will sing praises unto my God while I have any being.
Put not your trust in princes,
    Nor in the son of man in whom there is no help.
His breath goeth forth, he returneth to his earth;
    In that very day his thoughts perish.
Happy is he that hath the God of Jacob for his help,
    Whose hope is in the Lord his God:
Which made heaven and earth,
The sea, and all that therein is:
    Which keepeth truth for ever:
Which executeth judgment for the oppressed:
Which giveth food to the hungry.
    The Lord looseth the prisoners:
The Lord openeth the eyes of the blind:
The Lord raiseth them that are bowed down:
    The Lord loveth the righteous:
The Lord preserveth the strangers;
He relieveth the fatherless and widow:
    But the way of the wicked he turneth upside down.
The Lord shall reign for ever,
Even thy God, O Zion, unto all generations.
    Praise ye the Lord.

PSALM CXLVII.

Praise ye the Lord:
For it is good to sing praises unto our God;
    For it is pleasant; and praise is comely.
The Lord doth build up Jerusalem:
    He gathereth together the outcasts of Israel.
He healeth the broken in heart,
    And bindeth up their wounds.
He telleth the number of the stars;
    He calleth them all by their names.
Great is our Lord, and of great power:
    His understanding is infinite.
The Lord lifteth up the meek:
    He casteth the wicked down to the ground.
Sing unto the Lord with thanksgiving;
    Sing praise upon the harp unto our God:
Who covereth the heaven with clouds,
Who prepareth rain for the earth,
    Who maketh grass to grow upon the mountains.
He giveth to the beast his food,
    And to the young ravens which cry.
He delighteth not in the strength of the horse:
    He taketh not pleasure in the legs of a man.
The Lord taketh pleasure in them that fear him,
    In those that hope in his mercy.
Praise the Lord, O Jerusalem;
    Praise thy God, O Zion.
For he hath strengthened the bars of thy gates;
    He hath blessed thy children within thee.
He maketh peace in thy borders,
    And filleth thee with the finest of the wheat.

He sendeth forth his commandment upon earth:
His word runneth very swiftly.
He giveth snow like wool:
He scattereth the hoar-frost like ashes.
He casteth forth his ice like morsels:
Who can stand before his cold!
He sendeth out his word, and melteth them:
He causeth his wind to blow, and the waters flow.
He showeth his word unto Jacob,
His statutes and his judgments unto Israel.
He hath not dealt so with any nation:
And as for his judgments, they have not known them.
Praise ye the Lord.

PSALM CXLVIII.

Praise ye the Lord.
Praise ye the Lord from the heavens:
Praise him in the heights.
Praise ye him, all his angels:
Praise ye him, all his hosts.
Praise ye him, sun and moon:
Praise him, all ye stars of light.
Praise him, ye heavens of heavens.
And ye waters that be above the heavens.
Let them praise the name of the Lord:
For he commanded, and they were created:
He hath also established them for ever and ever:
He hath made a decree which shall not pass.
Praise the Lord from the earth,
Ye dragons, and all deeps:

Fire, and hail; snow and vapors;
> Stormy wind fulfilling his word:

Mountains, and all hills;
> Fruitful trees, and all cedars:

Beasts, and all cattle;
> Creeping things, and flying fowl:

Kings of the earth, and all people;
> Princes, and all judges of the earth:

Both young men, and maidens;
> Old men, and children:

Let them praise the name of the Lord:
For his name alone is excellent;
> His glory is above the earth and heaven.

He also exalteth the glory of his people,
> The praise of all his saints;

Even of the children of Israel, a people near unto him.
> Praise ye the Lord.

PSALM CXLIX.

Praise ye the Lord.
Sing unto the Lord a new song,
> And his praise in the congregation of saints.

Let Israel rejoice in him that made him:
> Let the children of Zion be joyful in their King.

Let them praise his name in the dance:
> Let them sing praises unto him with the timbrel and harp.

For the Lord taketh pleasure in his people:
> He will beautify the meek with salvation.

PSALM CL.

Praise ye the Lord.
Praise God in his sanctuary:
   Praise him in the firmament of his power.
Praise him for his mighty acts:
   Praise him according to his excellent greatness.
Praise him with the sound of the trumpet;
   Praise him with the psaltery and harp.
Praise him with the timbrel and dance;
   Praise him with stringed instruments and organs.
Praise him upon the loud cymbals:
   Praise him upon the high sounding cymbals.
Let every thing that hath breath praise the Lord.
   Praise ye the Lord.

HYMNS.

MORNING AND EVENING

1. *Morning Hymn.* 11s & 10s.

1 Now, when the dusky shades of night retreating,
   Before the sun's red banner swiftly flee;
Now, when the terrors of the dark are fleeting,
   O Lord! we lift our thankful hearts to thee.

2 To thee, whose word, the fount of life unsealing,
   When hill and dale in thickest darkness lay,
Awoke bright rays across the dim earth stealing,
   And bade the even and morn complete the day.

3 Look from the tower of heaven, and send to cheer us,
   Thy light and truth to guide us onward still;
Still let thy mercy as of old be near us,
   And lead us safely to thy holy hill.

4 So when that morn of endless light is waking,
   And shades of evil from its splendor flee,
Safe may we rise, the earth's dark breast forsaking,
   Through all the long bright day to dwell with thee.

2. *Morning Hymn.* C. M.

1 Now that the sun is beaming bright,
   Implore we, bending low,
That he, the uncreated Light,
   May guide us as we go.

2 No sinful word, nor deed of wrong,
  Nor thoughts that idly rove,
But simple truth be on our tongue,
  And in our hearts be love.

3 And while the hours in order flow,
  Securely keep, O God,
Our hearts, beleaguered by the foe,
  That tempts our every road.

4 And grant that to thine honor, Lord,
  Our daily toil may tend;
That we begin it at thy word,
  And in thy favor end.

3. *Prayer.* L. M.

1 Thou Brightness of the Father's ray,
True Light of light, and Day of day:
Light's fountain and eternal spring:
Thou Morn the morn illumining!

2 Glide in, thou very Sun divine;
With everlasting brightness shine:
And shed abroad on every sense
The Spirit's light and influence.

3 Thee, Father, let us seek aright:
The Father of perpetual light:
The Father of Almighty grace:
Each wile of sin away to chase.

4 Our acts with courage do thou fill:
Blunt thou the tempter's tooth of ill:
Misfortune into good convert,
Or give us grace to bear unhurt.

5 And Christ, our daily food be nigh,
And Faith our daily cup supply:

So may we quaff, to calm and bless,
The Spirit's rapturous holiness.

4. *" The day that God hath blessed."* H. M.

1 AWAKE, ye saints, awake!
   And hail this sacred day;
In loftiest songs of praise
   Your joyful homage pay:
Come, bless the day that God hath blest,
The type of heaven's eternal rest.

2 On this auspicious morn
   The Lord of life arose;
He burst the bars of death,
   And vanquished all our foes;
And now he pleads our cause above,
And reaps the fruit of all his love.

3 Hither, from earth's remotest end,
Lo! the redeemed of God ascend,
   Their tribute hither bring:
Here, crowned with everlasting joy,
In hymns of praise their tongues employ,
   And hail th' immortal King.

5. *The Morning and Evening Light.* L. M.

1 WHEN, streaming from the eastern skies,
The morning light salutes mine eyes,
O Sun of righteousness divine,
On me with beams of mercy shine!
Oh! chase the clouds of guilt away,
And turn my darkness into day.

2 When each day's scenes and labors close,
And wearied nature seeks repose,

With pard'ning mercy richly blest,
Guard me, my Father, while I rest;
And, as each morning sun shall rise,
Oh, lead me onward to the skies!

3 And at my life's last setting-sun,
My conflicts o'er, my labors done,
Father, thy heavenly radiance shed,
To cheer and bless my dying bed;
And, from death's gloom my spirit raise,
To see thy face, and sing thy praise.

6. *Prayer for the Fatherless.* 12s.

1 WHEN the sun gloriously comes forth from the ocean,
   Making earth beautiful, chasing shadows away,
Thus do we offer thee our prayer of devotion,
   God of the fatherless! guide us, guard us to-day.

2 When o'er the western hills, the sunset tints blending,
   Show us how quickly fades all that on earth seems bright,
Still to unfading realms our prayer is ascending,
   God of the fatherless! guide us, guard us to-night.

7. *Vesper Hymn.*

1 HARK! the vesper hymn is stealing,
   O'er the waters soft and clear;
Nearer yet, and nearer pealing,
   Now it bursts upon the ear!
      Jubilate. Amen.
Farther now, now farther stealing,
   Soft it fades upon the ear.

2 Now like moonlight waves retreating,
   To the shore it dies along;

EVENING.

Now like angry surges meeting,
  Breathes the mingled tide of song.
    Jubilate. Amen.
Hush! again like waves retreating,
  To the shore it dies along.

8.   *Vespers.*   P. M.

1 FADING, still fading, the last beam is shining;
Father in heaven! the day is declining;
Safety and innocence flee with the light,
Temptation and danger walk forth with the night;
From the fall of the shade till the morning bells chime,
Shield us from danger and keep us from crime!
Father! have mercy, through Jesus Christ our Lord!
    Amen!

2 Father in heaven! Oh, hear when we call,
Through Jesus Christ, who is Saviour of all!
Fainting and feeble, we trust in thy might;
In doubting and darkness thy love be our light!
Let us sleep on thy breast while the night taper burns,
And wake in thy arms when the morning returns.
Father! have mercy, through Jesus Christ our Lord!
    Amen!

9.   *Sabbath Evening.*   L. M.

1 SWEET is the light of Sabbath eve,
    And soft the sunbeams ling'ring there;
  For these blest hours the world I leave,
    Wafted on wings of faith and prayer.

2 Season of rest! the tranquil soul
    Feels the sweet calm, and melts in love;
  And while these sacred moments roll,
    Faith sees a smiling heaven above.

3 Nor will our days of toil be long:
  Our pilgrimage will soon be trod;
And we shall join the ceaseless song,
  The endless Sabbath of our God.

10. *Vespers.* 10s & 4s.

1 Father supreme! thou high and holy One,
    To thee we bow;
  Now, when the labor of the day is done,
    Devoutly, now.

2 From age to age unchanging, still the same,
    All-good thou art;
  Hallowed for ever be thy reverend name
    In every heart!

3 When the glad morn upon the hills was spread,
    Thy smile was there;
  Now, as the darkness gathers overhead,
    We feel thy care.

4 Night spreads her shade upon another day
    For ever past;
  So o'er our faults, thy love, we humbly pray,
    A veil may cast.

5 Silence and sleep, o'er hearts by earth distressed,
    Now sweetly steal;
  So every fear that struggles in the breast
    Shall faith conceal.

6 Thou through the dark wilt watch above our sleep
    With eye of love;
  And thou wilt wake us when the sunbeams peep
    The hills above.

7 Oh, may each heart its gratitude express
    As life expands,
  And find the triumph of its happiness
    In thy commands!

11. *The Departed.* P. M.

1 The spirits of the loved and the departed
   Are with us, and they tell us of the sky,
A rest for the bereaved and broken-hearted,
   A house not made with hands, a home on high;
Holy monitions,—a mysterious breath,—
   A whisper from the marble halls of death.

2 They have gone from us, and the grave is strong,
   Yet in night's silent watches they are near;
Their voices linger round us, as the song
   Of the sweet bird that lingers on the ear,
When, floating upward in the flush of even,
   Its form is lost from earth and swallowed up in heaven.

12. *Even Song.* 11s.

1 Be near us, O Father! through night's silent hour;
Impart to our slumbers thy calmness divine;
Drop rest on our lids like the dew on the flower,
That even our still sleep may have something of thine.

2 Oh, watch o'er our couch; drive the tempter away;
From the sins that corrupt and betray keep us free;
That nor fancy shall wander, nor passion shall stray,
And we dream not a thought that's displeasing to thee

3 And grant, when deep sleep o'er our senses shall close
That the heart may still watch, all unclouded and clear,
Guard, guard still thy children; and bless the repose
That, stainless of sin, is untouched by a fear.

4 Then still to thee, Father, our praises we pay;
Still to thee we will offer love's infinite store;
Send down thy pure Spirit, even now while we pray;
Be with us, and keep us, and bless evermore!

13. *Song in the Night.* 7s.

1 Slowly, by God's hand unfurled,
Down around the weary world
Falls the darkness; oh, how still
Is the working of his will!

2 Mighty Spirit, ever nigh!
Work in me as silently;
Veil the day's distracting sights,
Show me heaven's eternal lights.

3 Living stars to view be brought
In the boundless realms of thought,
High and infinite desires,
Flaming like those upper fires.

4 Holy truth, eternal right,
Let them break upon my sight;
Let them shine serene and still,
And with light my being fill.

14. *Evening Blessing.* 8s & 7s.

1 Holiest! breathe an evening blessing,
Ere repose our eyelids seal;
Sin and want we come confessing;
Thou canst save and thou canst heal.

2 Though destruction walk around us,
Though the arrows past us fly,
Angel guards from thee surround us—
We are safe if thou art nigh.

3 Though the night be dark and dreary,
Darkness cannot hide from thee;
Thou art He who, never weary,
Watcheth where thy people be.

EVENING.

4 Should swift death this night o'ertake us,
  And our couch become our tomb,
May the morn in heaven awake us,
  Clad in bright and deathless bloom.

15. *Dona nobis pacem.* P. M.

1 HEAR us, Heavenly Father, hear us!
  Give to us thy perfect peace,
  Thou whose love unsleeping
  Watch is ever keeping.
  Shades of evening gather;
  Thou, our heavenly Father,
  Holy and Merciful,
  Hear our evening prayer!

2 When life's glooms o'ertake us,
  Thou wilt not forsake us:
  When life's shadows darken,
  Then our cry wilt hearken;
  Holy and Merciful!
  Thou wilt hear our prayer.
  Give us thy peace, O Lord!
  Keep us in thy perfect peace.

16. *Nox et tenebræ.* L. M.

1 AGAIN, as evening's shadow falls,
  We gather in these hallowed walls,
  And vesper Hymn and vesper Prayer
  Rise mingling on the holy air.
  May struggling hearts, that seek release,
  Here find the rest of God's own peace;
  And, strengthened here by Hymn and Prayer,
  Lay down the burden and the care!

2 O God, our Light, to thee we bow!
  Within all shadows, standest thou:

Give deeper calm than night can bring,
Give sweeter songs than lips can sing!
Life's tumult we must meet again,
We cannot at the shrine remain;
But, in the spirit's secret cell,
May Hymn and Prayer for ever dwell!

17. *Lucis Creator optime.* L. M.

1 O BLEST Creator of the light!
   Who didst the dawn from darkness bring,
And in the heaven's glorious height
   Didst bid the stars together sing:
Who, gently blending eve with morn
   And morn with eve, didst call them day;
Thick flows the flood of darkness down,
   Oh, hear us as we come to pray!

2 Keep thou our souls from thought of crime;
   Keep them from guilt's remorseful strife;
Not living for the things of time,
   But living the eternal life.
Teach us to knock at heaven's high door;
   Teach us the prize of life to win;
Teach us all evil to abhor,
   And purify ourselves within.

18. *Nearer to Thee.* P. M.

1 NEARER, my God, to thee,
   Nearer to thee!
E'en though it be a cross
   That raiseth me;
Still all my song shall be —
Nearer, my God, to thee,
   Nearer to thee!

2 Though, like the wanderer,
    The sun gone down,
  Darkness be over me,
    My rest a stone;
  Yet in my dreams I'd be
  Nearer, my God, to thee,—
    Nearer to thee!

3 There let the way appear,
    Steps unto heaven;
  All that thou sendest me,
    In mercy given;
  Angels to beckon me
  Nearer, my God, to thee,—
    Nearer to thee!

4 Then with my waking thoughts,
    Bright with thy praise,
  Out of my stony griefs,
    Bethel I'll raise;
  So by my woes to be
  Nearer, my God, to thee,—
    Nearer to thee!

5 Or if on joyful wing,
    Cleaving the sky,
  Sun, moon, and stars forgot,
    Upward I fly,
  Still all my song shall be,
  Nearer my God, to thee,—
    Nearer to thee!

19. *Evening Meditations.* C. M.

1 Behold the western evening light!
    It melts in deepening gloom;
  So calmly Christians sink away,
    Descending to the tomb.

The winds breathe low,—the withering leaf
  Scarce whispers from the tree;
So gently flows the parting breath,
  When good men cease to be.

2 How beautiful, on all the hills,
  The crimson light is shed!
'Tis like the peace the Christian gives
  To mourners round his bed.
How mildly on the wandering cloud
  The sunset beam is cast!
'Tis like the memory left behind,
  When loved ones breathe their last.

3 And now above the dews of night
  The yellow star appears;
So faith springs in the hearts of those
  Whose eyes are bathed in tears.
But soon the morning's happier light
  Its glories shall restore;
And eyelids that are sealed in death
  Shall wake to close no more.

20. *Christmas Vesper Hymn.* P. M.

1 DEPART awhile, each thought of care,
  Be earthly things forgotten all,
And speak, my soul, thy vesper prayer,
  Obedient to that sacred call.
For hark! the pealing chorus swells,
  Devotion chants the hymn of praise,
And now of joy and hope it tells,
  Till fainting on the ear, it says—
    Glory be to thee, our Lord,
    Our Lord, our Lord.

2 Thine, wondrous babe of Galilee,
  Fond theme of David's harp and song,

Thine are the notes of minstrelsy,
  To thee its ransomed chords belong.
And hark! again the chorus swells,
  The song is wafted on the breeze,
And to the listening earth it tells,
  In accents soft and sweet as these—
    Glory be to thee, our Lord.

3 My heart doth feel that still he's near,
  To meet the soul in hours like this,
Else, why, O why, that falling tear,
  When all is peace and love and bliss.
But hark! that pealing chorus swells
  Anew its thrilling vesper strain,
And still of joy and hope it tells,
  And bids creation sing again—
    Glory be to thee, our Lord.

21.   *Evening Aspiration.*   7s & 6s.

1 THE mellow eve is gliding
    Serenely down the west;
So, every care subsiding,
    My soul would sink to rest.

2 The woodland hum is ringing
    The daylight's gentle close;
May angels, round me singing,
    Thus hymn my last repose.

3 The evening star has lighted
    Her crystal lamp on high;
So, when in death benighted,
    May hope illume the sky.

4 In golden splendor dawning,
    The morrow's light shall break:
Oh! on the last bright morning,
    May I in glory wake.

EVENING.

22. *Twilight Hymn.* 12s & 11s.

1 See, daylight is fading o'er earth and o'er ocean,
    The sun has gone down on the far distant sea;
Oh! now, in the hush of the fitful commotion,
    We lift our tired spirits, blest Saviour, to thee.

2 Full oft wast thou found afar on the mountain
    As eventide spread her dark wing o'er the wave:
Thou Son of the Highest, and life's endless fountain,
    Be with us, we pray thee, to bless and to save.

3 And oft as the tumult of life's heaving billow
    Shall toss our frail bark, driving wild o'er night's deep,
Let thy healing wing be stretched o'er our pillow,
    And guard us from evil, though death watch our sleep.

4 To God, our great Father, whose throne is in heaven,
    Who dwells with the lowly and humble in heart,
Through thy Son let all honor and glory be given;
    One God, ever blessed and praised, thou art.

23. *Entire Trust.* L. M.

1 Rocked in the cradle of the deep,
    I lay me down in peace to sleep;
    Secure I rest upon the wave,
    For thou, O Lord, hast power to save.

2 I know thou wilt not slight my call,
    For thou dost mark the sparrow's fall!
    And calm and peaceful is my sleep,
    Rocked in the cradle of the deep.

3 And such the trust that still were mine,
    Though stormy winds swept o'er the brine,
    Or though the tempest's fiery breath
    Roused from sleep to wreck and death!

4 In ocean caves still safe with thee,
  The germs of immortality;
  And calm and peaceful is my sleep,
  Rocked in the cradle of the deep.

24. *Vespers.* L. M.

Thee in the hymns of morn we praise,
To thee our voice at eve we raise;
Oh, grant us, with thy saints on high,
Thee through all time to glorify.

25. *Salutis humanæ sator.* L. M.

1 O thou pure Light of souls that love,
    True joy of every human breast,
  Sower of life's immortal seed,
    Our Saviour and Redeemer blest!

2 Be thou our guide, be thou our goal,
    Be thou our pathway to the skies;
  Our joy when sorrow fills the soul,
    In death our everlasting prize.

26. *Vespers.* P. M.

1   The day expires!
      My soul desires
    And pants to see that day
 When whate'er hath vexed her here
      Shall be done away.

2   The night is here!
      Oh! be thou near;
  Lord, make it light within;
 Drive away from out my heart
      All the night of sin.

EVENING.

3 The sunbeams pale,
And flee and fail.
O uncreated Sun!
Let thy light now shine on us,
Then our joy were won.

4 All things that move
Below, above,
Now with sleep are blest;
Work thou still in me while I
Calmly in thee rest.

5 When shall the sway
Of night and day
Cease to rule man thus?
When that brightest of days
Once shall dawn on us.

6 Oh! never then
Her light again
Jerusalem shall miss;
For the Lamb shall be her light,
Filling her with bliss.

27.   *Evening Prayer.*   P. M.

1 'Tis Nature's time for prayer—
The silent praises of the glorious sky,
And the earth's orisons, profound and high,
To Heaven their breathings bear.

2 With them my soul would bend
In humble rev'rence at thy holy throne,
Trusting thy mercy in thy Son alone
Thy sceptre to extend.

3 If I this day have striven
With thy blest Spirit, or have bowed the knee
To aught of earth in weak idolatry,
I pray to be forgiven.

4   If I have turned away
From grief or suff'ring which I might relieve,
Careless the cup of water e'en to give,
    Forgive me, Lord, I pray.

5   Father! my soul would be
Pure as the drops of eve's unsullied dew;
And as the stars, whose nightly course is true,
    So would I be to thee.

6   And now, O Father! take
The heart I cast with humble faith on thee,
And cleanse its depths from each impurity,
    For thine own mercy's sake!

28. *The Light Unchanging.*   8s & 7s.

1 Glorious God, we come to bless thee,
    Now when day is veiled in night;
Thou who knowest no beginning,
    Thou, the never-failing Light!

2 Thou the darkness hast dissolvèd,
    And the outward light created,
        That all things in light might be;
Fixing the unfixèd chaos,
    Moulding it to wondrous beauty,
        Into the fair world we see.

3 Thou enlightenest man with reason,
    Far beyond thy creatures dumb,
That light in thy Light beholding,
    Wholly light he might become.

4 Thou hast set the radiant heavens
    With thy many lamps of brightness,
        Filling all the vaults above,
Day and night in turn subjecting
    To a brotherhood of service,
        And a mutual law of love.

5 By the night our wearied nature,
   Resting from its toil and tears;
To the works, Lord, that thou lovest,
   Waking us when day appears.

29. *Trust in God.* P. M.

1 The night is come, wherein at last we rest,
God order this and all things for the best!
Beneath his blessing, fearless may we lie,
    Since he is nigh.

2 Drive evil thoughts and spirits far away;
O Father, watch o'er us till dawning day,
Body and soul alike from harm defend,
    Thine angels send.

3 Let holy prayers and thoughts our latest be,
Let us awake with joy, still close to thee;
In all serve thee; in every deed and thought
    Thy praise be sought.

4 Give to the sick, as thy beloved, sleep;
And help the captive, comfort those who weep;
Care for the widows' and the orphans' woe;
    Keep far our foe.

5 Father, thy Name be praised, thy kingdom come,
Thy will be wrought as in our heavenly home;
Keep us in life, forgive our sins, deliver
    Us now and ever! Amen.

30. *Hymn of Trust.* L. M.

1 O Love Divine, that stooped to share
   Our sharpest pang, our bitterest tear,
On Thee we cast each earth-born care,
   We smile at pain while Thou art near!

2 Though long the weary way we tread,
    And sorrow crown each lingering year,
No path we shun, no darkness dread,
    Our hearts still whispering, Thou art near!

3 When drooping pleasure turns to grief,
    And trembling faith is changed to fear,
The murmuring wind, the quivering leaf,
    Shall softly tell us, Thou art near!

4 On thee we fling our burdening woe,
    O Love Divine, for ever dear,
Content to suffer while we know,
    Living and dying, Thou art near!

31. *Easter.— Vespers.* P. M.

1 SMILE praises, O sky,
    Soft breathe them, O air,
Below, and on high,
    And everywhere!
The black troop of storms
    Has yielded to calm;
Tufted blossoms are peeping,
    And early palm.

2 Arouse thee, O spring;
    Ye flowers, come forth;
With thousand hues tinting
    The soft green earth:
Ye violets tender,
    And sweet roses bright,
Gay Lent-lilies blended
    With pure lilies white.

3 Sweep, tides of rich music,
    The full veins along;
And pour in full measure,
    Sweet voices, your song.

Sing, sing, for He liveth,
  He lives, as He said;
The Lord has arisen
  Unharmed from the dead.

4 Clap, clap your hands, mountains;
  Ye valleys, resound:
Leap, leap for joy, fountains;
  Ye hills, catch the sound.
All triumph! He liveth,
  He lives, as He said;
The Lord hath arisen
  Unharmed from the dead.

32. *Vesper Hymn.*

1 LORD of eternal purity!
  Who dost the world with light adorn,
And paint the tracts of azure sky
  With lovely hues of eve and morn:

2 Who didst command the sun to light
  His fiery wheel's effulgent blaze;
Didst set the moon her circuit bright;
  The stars their ever-winding maze:

3 That, each within its ordered sphere,
  They might divide the night from day;
And of the seasons through the year,
  The well-remembered signs display:

4 Scatter our night, eternal God,
  And kindle thy pure beam within;
Free us from guilt's oppressive load,
  And break the deadly bonds of sin.

33. *Sunset.* P. M.

1 The sun is set. I mark the stars as gleaming, one by
    one,
  Bright through the twilight's deepening shade the gems
    of evening shone;
  Till rising o'er the eastern hills the full-orbed moon is
    seen,
  And in her brightness walking forth along the blue
    serene.

2 And oh, while these fair works of thine possess my
    raptured thought,
  The moon which thy right hand hath formed, the stars
    thy fingers wrought;
  Lord, what is man, I cry, that thou a glance on him
    shouldst throw;
  Or son of man, that thou from heaven shouldst visit
    him below?

3 O'er him the solitude of night and stillness soon shall
    creep,
  As o'er this fading face of things, and mantle him in
    sleep;
  But thou hast said, we shall not sleep in everlasting
    night,
  But in the twinkling of an eye shall wake again to
    light.

4 Grant that each evening in its course this wayward
    heart may find,
  Still more observant of thy laws, and to thy will re-
    signed;
  And when the last dread evening comes, do thou my
    soul convey,
  With thee among thy saints to dwell in never-ending
    day!

GOD.

34. *A Sunday Hymn.* L. M.

1 Lord of all being throned afar,
Thy glory flames from sun and star;
Centre and soul of every sphere,
Yet to each loving heart how near?

2 Sun of our life, thy quickening ray
Sheds on our path the glow of day;
Star of our hope, thy softened light
Cheers the long watches of the night.

3 Our midnight is thy smile withdrawn;
Our noontide is thy gracious dawn;
Our rainbow arch thy mercy's sign;
All, save the clouds of sin, are thine!

4 Lord of all life, below, above,
Whose light is truth, whose warmth is love,
Before thy ever-blazing throne
We ask no lustre of our own.

5 Grant us thy truth to make us free,
And kindling hearts that burn for thee,
Till all thy living altars claim
One holy light, one heavenly flame!

35. *Wonders of God's Condescension.* 7s.

1 Hallelujah! raise, oh, raise
To our God the song of praise:
All his servants join to sing,
God, our Saviour and our King.

2 Blessed be for evermore
That dread name which we adore:

O'er all nations, God alone,
Higher than the heavens his throne.

3 Yet to view the heavens he bends;
Yea, to earth he condescends;
Passing by the rich and great,
For the low and desolate.

4 He can raise the poor to stand
With the princes of the land;
Wealth upon the needy shower,
Set the lowliest high in power.

5 He the broken spirit cheers,
Turns to joy the mourner's tears;
Such the wonders of his ways:
Praise his name, forever praise.

36. *The Spirit of a little Child.* C. M.

1 Father, I know that all my life
  Is portioned out for me;
The changes that will surely come
  I do not fear to see:
I ask thee for a present mind,
  Intent on pleasing thee.

2 I ask thee for a thoughtful love,
  Through constant watching wise,
To meet the glad with joyful smiles,
  And wipe the weeping eyes;
A heart at leisure from itself,
  To soothe and sympathize.

3 I ask thee for the daily strength,
  To none that ask denied,
A mind to blend with outward life,
  While keeping at thy side;
Content to fill a little space,
  If thou be glorified.

4 And if some things I do not ask,
  Among my blessings be,
I'd have my spirit filled the more
  With grateful love to thee;
More careful—not to serve thee much,
  But please thee perfectly.

37. *An ancient Hymn of Praise to God.* L. M.

1 Thee we adore, eternal Lord!
  We praise thy name with one accord;
  Thy saints, who here thy goodness see,
  Through all the world do worship thee.

2 To thee aloud all angels cry,
  The heavens and all the powers on high:
  Thee, holy, holy, holy King,
  Lord God of hosts they ever sing.

3 Th' apostles join the glorious throng;
  The prophets swell th' immortal song;
  The martyrs' noble army raise
  Eternal anthems to thy praise.

4 From day to day, O Lord, do we
  Highly exalt and honor thee!
  Thy name we worship and adore,
  World without end for evermore!

5 Vouchsafe, O Lord, we humbly pray,
  To keep us safe from sin this day;
  Have mercy, Lord! we trust in thee;
  Oh, let us ne'er confounded be!

38. *"Who is like unto the Lord our God."* 10s & 11s.

1 Oh, worship the King, all glorious above;
  Oh, gratefully sing his power and his love!

Our Shield and Defender, the Ancient of days;
Pavilioned in splendor, and girded with praise.

2 Oh, tell of his might, oh, sing of his grace,
Whose robe is the light, whose canopy space!
His chariots of wrath the deep thunder-clouds form,
And dark is his path on the wings of the storm.

3 Thy bountiful care what tongue can recite?
It breathes in the air, it shines in the light,
It streams from the hills, it descends to the plains,
And sweetly distils in the dew and the rains.

4 Frail children of dust, and feeble as frail,
In thee do we trust, nor find thee to fail;
Thy mercies how tender! how firm to the end!
Our Maker, Defender, Redeemer, and Friend.

39. *"God is Love."* 8s & 7s.

1 God is love; his mercy brightens
All the path in which we rove;
Bliss he wakes, and woe he lightens:
God is wisdom, God is love.

2 Chance and change are busy ever;
Man decays, and ages move:
But his mercy waneth never,
God is wisdom, God is love.

3 Even the hour that darkest seemeth,
Will his changeless goodness prove;
From the gloom his brightness streameth:
God is wisdom, God is love.

4 He with earthly cares entwineth
Hope and comfort from above:
Everywhere his glory shineth,
God is wisdom, God is love.

40. *"The Lord is my salvation; whom shall I fear?"* 7s & 6s.

1 God is my strong salvation;
  What foe have I to fear?
In darkness and temptation,
  My Light, my Help, is near.

2 Though hosts encamp around me,
  Firm in the fight I stand;
What terror can confound me,
  With God at my right hand?

3 Place on the Lord reliance;
  My soul, with courage wait;
His truth be thy affiance,
  When faint and desolate.

4 His might thy heart shall strengthen,
  His love thy joy increase;
Mercy thy days shall lengthen,
  The Lord will give thee peace!

41. *Prayer for the Father's guidance.* 8s & 7s.

1 Gently, Lord! oh, gently lead us
  Through this lonely vale of tears;
Through the changes thou'st decreed us,
  Till our last great change appears:
When temptation's darts assail us,
  When in devious paths we stray,
Let thy goodness never fail us,
  Lead us in thy perfect way.

2 In the hour of pain and anguish,
  In the hour when death draws near,
Suffer not our hearts to languish,
  Suffer not our souls to fear:

And, when mortal life is ended,
  Bid us on thy bosom rest;
Till, by angel bands attended,
  We awake among the blest.

42. *God's Providence.* 7s.

1 CHILDREN of God lack nothing,
    His promise bears them through;
  Who gives the lilies clothing,
    Will clothe his people too.
  Beneath the spreading heavens
    No creature but is fed;
  And he who feeds the ravens
    Will give his children bread.

2 Though vine and fig-tree neither
    Their wonted fruit should bear;
  Though all the field should wither,
    Nor flocks nor herds be there;
  Yet God the same abiding,
    His praise shall tune my voice,
  For while in him confiding,
    I cannot but rejoice.

43. *Longing for rest in God.* 7s & 6s.

1 O ALMIGHTY God of love!
    Thy holy arm display;
  Send us succor from above,
    Against the evil day;
  Arm our weakness with thy power,
  Put thy strength our hearts within,
  Be our stronghold and our tower,
    Against the assaults of sin.

2 Could we of thy strength take hold,
    And always feel thee near,

Confident, divinely bold,
  Our souls would know no fear.
Nothing could their firmness shock;
Though the gates of hell assail,
Were we built upon the rock,
  They never could prevail.

3 Thou wouldst, in the trying hour,
  A sure protection be,
Guard us from temptation's power,
  And fix our souls on thee.
Lord, on thee our trust is placed,
Never thence may we remove,
In the arms of love embraced,
  Thine everlasting love.

44. *The Penitent Son.* C. M.

1 O, RICHLY, Father, have I been
  Blest evermore by thee!
And morning, noon, and night thou hast
  Preserved me tenderly.

2 And yet the love which thou shouldst claim
  To idols I have given;
Too oft have bound to earth the hopes
  That know no home but heaven.

3 Unworthy to be called thy son,
  I come with shame to thee,
Father!—O, more than Father, thou
  Hast always been to me!

4 Help me to break the heavy chains
  The world has round me thrown,
And know the glorious liberty
  Of an obedient son.

5 That I may henceforth heed whate'er
  Thy voice within me saith,

Fix deeply in my heart of hearts
A principle of faith,—

6 Faith that, like armor to my soul,
Shall keep all evil out,
More mighty than an angel host,
Encamping round about.

45. *The Light of Life.* 7s.

1 Light of life, seraphic fire!
Love divine thyself impart:
Every fainting soul inspire;
Enter every drooping heart:
Every mournful spirit cheer,
Scatter all our doubt and gloom;
Father, in thy grace appear,
To thy human temples come!

2 Come in this accepted hour,
Bring thy heavenly kingdom in;
Fill us with thy glorious power,
Rooting out the seeds of sin:
Nothing more can we require,
We can rest in nothing less:
Be thou all our heart's desire,
All our joy and all our peace.

46. *Prayer of a Stricken People.* 7s & 6s.

1 O Thou whose power stupendous
Upholds the earth and sky,
Thy grace preserving send us—
To thee, O Lord! we cry.

2 From wilds of fearful error,
Wherein we darkly stray,
Oppressed with doubt and terror
For saving aid we pray.

3 O God of mercy, hear us!
   Our pain, our sorrow, see;
Thy healing pity spare us,
   And bring us home to thee!

47. *God everywhere present.* 7s.

1 They who seek the throne of grace
Find that throne in every place!
If we live a life of prayer,
God is present everywhere.

2 In our sickness and our health,
In our want, or in our wealth,
If we look to God in prayer,
God is present everywhere.

3 When our earthly comforts fail,
When the woes of life prevail,
'Tis the time for earnest prayer;—
God is present everywhere.

4 Then, my soul, in every strait
To thy Father come, and wait;
He will answer every prayer;—
God is present everywhere.

48. *Coming together in the Name of Jesus.* L. M.

1 Great God! the followers of thy Son,
   We bow before thy mercy-seat,
To worship thee, the holy one,
   And pour our wishes at thy feet.

2 Oh, grant thy blessing here to-day!
   Oh, give thy people joy and peace!
The tokens of thy love display,
   And favor, that shall never cease.

3 We seek the truth which Jesus brought;
His path of light we long to tread;
Here be his holy doctrines taught,
And here their purest influence shed.

4 May faith, and hope, and love abound;
Our sins and errors be forgiven;
And we, from day to day, be found
Children of God, and heirs of heaven.

49. *Christian Love.* 7s.

1 FATHER! we look up to thee;
Let us in thy love agree;
Thou, who art the God of peace,
Bid contention ever cease.

2 Make us of one heart and mind,
Self-forgetful, true, and kind;
Strong, yet meek in thought and word,
Like thy Son, our blessed Lord.

3 Let us for each other care,
Each the other's burden bear;
Ready, when reviled, to bless,
Studious of the law of peace.

4 Father! all our souls inspire,
Fill us with love's sacred fire;
Guided by that blessed light,
Order all our steps aright.

5 Free from anger, free from pride,
Let us thus in thee abide;
All the depths of love express,—
All the heights of holiness.

50. *Lord, have mercy.* 7s.

1 Lord, have mercy when we pray
Strength to seek a better way;
When our wakening thoughts begin
First to loathe their cherished sin;
When our weary spirits fail,
And our aching brows are pale;
Then thy strengthening grace afford;
Then, oh, then, have mercy, Lord!

2 Lord, have mercy when we know
First how vain this world below;
When its darker thoughts oppress,
Doubts perplex, and fears distress;
When the earliest gleam is given
Of the bright but distant heaven;
Then thy strengthening grace afford;
Then, oh, then, have mercy, Lord!

51. *Quiet Worship.* 7s & 6s.

1 Open, Lord, mine inward ear,
   And bid my heart rejoice;
Bid my quiet spirit hear
   The comfort of thy voice;
Never in the whirlwind found,
Or where earthquakes rock the place,
Still and silent is the sound,
   The whisper of thy grace.

2 From the world of sin, and noise,
   And hurry, I withdraw;
For the small and inward voice
   I wait with humble awe;

Silent am I now and still,
Will not in thy presence move;
To my waiting soul reveal
The secret of thy love!

52.   *The Angels of Grief.*   11s & 4s.

1 With silence only as their benediction,
    God's angels come
Where, in the shadow of a great affliction,
    The soul sits dumb.

2 Yet would we say, what every heart approveth,—
    Our Father's will,
Calling to him the dear ones whom he loveth,
    Is mercy still.

3 Not upon us or ours the solemn angel
    Hath evil wrought;
The funeral anthem is a glad evangel;
    The good die not!

4 God calls our loved ones, but we lose not wholly
    What he has given;
They live on earth, in thought and deed, as truly
    As in his heaven.

53.   *Every Place a Temple.*   L. M.

1 O Thou to whom, in ancient time,
    The lyre of Hebrew bards was strung,
Whom kings adored in songs sublime,
    And prophets praised with glowing tongue:

2 Not now on Zion's height alone
    Thy favored worshippers may dwell;
Nor where, at sultry noon, thy Son
    Sat, weary, by the patriarch's well.

3 From every place below the skies,
   The grateful song, the fervent prayer,—
The incense of the heart,—may rise
   To heaven, and find acceptance there.

4 To thee shall age, with snowy hair,
   And strength, and beauty, bend the knee;
And childhood lisp, with reverent air,
   Its praises and its prayers to thee.

5 O Thou to whom, in ancient time,
   The lyre of prophet bards was strung,
To thee, at last, in every clime,
   Shall temples rise, and praise be sung!

54. *Supplication.* S. M.

1 THE praying spirit breathe,
   The watching power impart,
From all entanglements beneath
   Call off my peaceful heart:
My feeble mind sustain,
   By worldly thoughts oppressed;
Appear, and bid me turn again
   To my eternal rest.

2 Swift to my rescue come,
   Thy own this moment seize;
Gather my wandering spirit home,
   And keep in perfect peace:
Suffered no more to rove
   O'er all the earth abroad,
Arrest the prisoner of thy love,
   And shut me up in God.

55. *For Help in Weakness.* 8s & 7s

1 LORD, with fervor I would praise thee
   For the bliss thy love bestows,

For the pardoning grace that saves me,
  And the peace that from it flows:
Help, O God, my weak endeavor;
  This dull soul to rapture raise;
Thou must light the flame, or never
  Can my love be warmed to praise.

2 Praise, my soul, the God that sought thee,
  Wretched wanderer, far astray,
Found thee lost, and kindly brought thee
  From the paths of death away;
Praise, with love's devoutest feeling,
  Him who saw thy guilt-born fear,
And, the light of hope revealing,
  Bade the blood-stained cross appear.

3 Lord, this bosom's ardent feeling
  Vainly would my lips express;
Low before thy footstool kneeling,
  Deign thy suppliant's prayer to bless.
Let thy grace, my soul's chief treasure,
  Love's pure flame within me raise,
And, since words can never measure,
  Let my life show forth thy praise.

56. *Guide us in Life and Death.* 8s, 7s & 4s.

1 Guide me, O thou great Jehovah,
  Pilgrim through this barren land;
I am weak, but thou art mighty;
  Hold me with thy powerful hand:
    Bread of heaven!
  Feed me till I want no more.

2 Open now the crystal fountains
  Whence the living waters flow;
Let the fiery, cloudy pillar
  Lead me all my journey through:

Strong Deliverer!
Be thou still my strength and shield.

3 When I tread the verge of Jordan,
Bid my anxious fears subside;
Bear me through the swelling current,
Land me safe on Canaan's side:
Songs of praises
I will ever give to thee.

57. *Asking God's Pity and Grace.* C. M.

1 O God, whose dread and dazzling brow
Love never yet forsook,
On those who seek thy presence now
In deep compassion look.

2 For many a frail and erring heart
Is in thy holy sight,
And feet too willing to depart
From the plain way of right.

3 Yet, pleased the humble prayer to hear,
And kind to all that live,
Thou, when thou seest the contrite tear,
Art ready to forgive.

4 Lord, aid us, with thy heavenly grace,
Our truest bliss to find,
Nor sternly judge our erring race,
So feeble and so blind.

58. *"Lift up your hearts."* C. M.

1 "Lift up your hearts!" Yes, I will lift
My heart and soul, dear Lord to thee,
Who every good and perfect gift
Vouchsaf'st so lavishly and free.

2 All that is best from thee comes down
  On us, with rich and ample store,
Thy bounteous hands our wishes crown
  With good, increasing more and more.

3 'Twas thou that gave us life and breath,
  It is thy hand that holds us still,
That keeps us from the sleep of death,
  And shelters us from every ill.

4 All thou hast given is thine, then take
  Me, thine own gift, for all thine own,
And teach me every day to make
  New vows of love to thee alone.

59. *My God and my all.* P. M.

1 While thou, O my God, art my help and defender,
    No cares can o'erwhelm me, no terrors appall;
  The wiles and the snares of this world will but render
    More lively my hope in my God and my all.

2 Yes; thou art my refuge in sorrow and danger;
    My strength when I suffer; my hope when I fall;
  My comfort and joy in this land of the stranger;
    My treasure, my glory, my God, and my all.

3 To thee, dearest Lord, will I turn without ceasing,
    Though grief may oppress me, or sorrow befall;
  And love thee, till death, my blest spirit releasing,
    Secures me my Saviour, my God, and my all.

4 And when thou demandest the life thou hast given,
    With joy will I answer thy merciful call;
  And quit thee on earth, but to find thee in heaven,
    My portion for ever, my God, and my all.

60. *God seen in all things.* L. M.

1 Thou art, O God, the life and light
  Of all this wondrous world we see;
Its glow by day, its smile by night,
  Are but reflections caught from thee;
Where'er we turn, thy glories shine,
And all things fair and bright are thine.

2 When day, with farewell beam, delays,
  Among the opening clouds of even,
And we can almost think we gaze
  Through golden vistas into heaven,
Those hues that make the sun's decline
So soft, so radiant, Lord, are thine.

3 When night, with wings of starry gloom,
  O'ershadows all the earth and skies,
Like some dark, beauteous bird, whose plume
  Is sparkling with unnumbered eyes,—
That sacred gloom, those fires divine,
So grand, so countless, Lord, are thine.

4 When youthful spring around us breathes,
  Thy spirit warms her fragrant sigh,
And every flower the summer wreathes,
  Is born beneath thy kindling eye;
Where'er we turn, thy glories shine,
And all things fair and bright are thine.

61. *Hear our Prayer.* P. M.

1   Hear, Father, hear our prayer!
Thou who art Pity where sorrow prevaileth,
Thou who art Safety when mortal help faileth,
  Strength to the feeble, and Hope to despair,
    Hear, Father, hear our prayer!

2   Hear, Father, hear our prayer!
Wandering unknown in the land of the stranger,
Be with all travellers in sickness or danger,
  Guard thou their path, guide their feet from the
    snare:
    Hear, Father, hear our prayer!

3   Hear, Father, hear our prayer!
Still thou the tempest, night's terrors revealing,
In lightning flashing, in thy thunder pealing;
  Save thou the shipwrecked, the voyager spare:
    Hear, Father, hear our prayer.

4   Hear thou the poor that cry!
Feed thou the hungry, and lighten their sorrow,
Grant them the sunshine of hope for the morrow:
  They are thy children, their trust is on high:
    Hear thou the poor that cry!

5   Dry thou the mourner's tear!
Heal thou the wounds of time-hallowed affection:
Grant to the widow and orphan protection;
  Be in their trouble a friend ever near:
    Dry thou the mourner's tear!

6   Hear, Father, hear our prayer!
Long hath thy goodness our footsteps attended;
Be with the pilgrim whose journey is ended;
  When, at thy summons, for death we prepare,
    Hear, Father, hear our prayer!

62. *Homage to God from his works.*   7s.

1 HERALDS of creation! cry:
Praise the Lord, the Lord most high;
Heaven and earth! obey the call;
Praise the Lord, the Lord of all.

2 For he spake, and forth from night
Sprang the universe to light;

He commanded;—nature heard,
And stood fast upon his word.

3 Praise him, all ye hosts above,
Spirits perfected in love!
Sun and moon, your voices raise;
Sing, ye stars, your Maker's praise!

4 Earth, from all thy depth below,
Ocean's hallelujahs flow;
Lightning, vapor, wind, and storm,
Hail and snow, his will perform.

5 Vales and mountains burst in song;
Rivers roll with praise along!
Birds on wings of rapture soar,
Warble at his temple-door!

6 High above all height his throne;
Excellent his Name alone:
Him let all his works confess;
Him let every being bless.

JESUS CHRIST.

63. *Birth of Jesus.* 11s & 10s.

1 BRIGHTEST and best of the sons of the morning,
Dawn on our darkness and lend us thine aid;
Star of the East, the horizon adorning,
Guide where the infant Redeemer is laid.

2 Cold on his cradle the dew-drops are shining;
Low lies his head with the beasts of the stall;
Angels bend o'er him, in slumber reclining,—
Monarch, Redeemer, Restorer of all.

3 Say, shall we yield him, in costly devotion,
   Odors of Edom, and offerings divine?
Gems of the mountain, and pearls of the ocean,
   Myrrh from the forest, or gold from the mine?

4 Vainly we offer each ample oblation,
   Vainly with gold would his favor secure;
Richer by far is the heart's adoration;
   Dearer to God are the prayers of the poor.

64.   *Kingdom of Christ.*   7s & 6s.

1 Hail to the Lord's Anointed,
   Great David's greater Son;
Hail, in the time appointed,
   His reign on earth begun.
He comes to break oppression,
   To set the captive free,
To take away transgression,
   And rule in equity.

2 Before him on the mountains,
   Shall Peace, the herald, go;
And righteousness in fountains
   From hill to valley flow.
For him shall prayer unceasing,
   And daily vows ascend;
His kingdom still increasing,
   A kingdom without end.

3 O'er every foe victorious,
   He on his throne shall rest;
From age to age more glorious,
   All blessing and all blest.
The tide of time shall never
   His covenant remove;
His name shall stand for ever;
   That name to us is Love.

65. *"Did not our hearts burn within us?"*

1 Hath not thy heart within thee burned
  At evening's calm and holy hour,
As if its inmost depths discerned
  The presence of a loftier power?

2 As they, who once with Jesus trod,
  With kindling breast his accents heard,
But knew not that the Son of God
  Was uttering every burning word,—

3 Father of Jesus, thus thy voice
  Speaks to our hearts in tones divine;
Our spirits tremble and rejoice,
  But know not that the voice is thine.

4 Still be thy hallowed accents near;
  To doubt and passion whisper peace;
Direct us on our journey here,
  And bid, in heaven, our wanderings cease.

66. *Birth of Christ.*

1 It came upon the midnight clear,
  That glorious song of old,
From angels bending near the earth,
  To touch their harps of gold:—
"Peace on the earth—good will to men
  From heaven's all-gracious King"—
The world in solemn stillness lay
  To hear the angels sing.

2 Still through the cloven skies they come
  With peaceful wings unfurled,
And still their heavenly music floats
  O'er all the weary world;

Above its sad and lonely plains
  They bend on heavenly wing,
And ever o'er its Babel sounds
  The blessed angels sing.

3 For lo! the days are hastening on,
  By prophet bards foretold,
When with the ever-circling years,
  Comes round the age of gold;
When peace shall over all the earth
  Its ancient splendors fling,
And the whole world send back the song
  Which now the angels sing.

67. *Christ our Refuge.* 7s.

1 Jesus, lover of my soul,
  Let me to thy bosom fly,
While the nearer waters roll,
  While the tempest still is high:
Hide me, O my Saviour, hide,
  Till the storm of life be past;
Safe into the haven guide;
  Oh, receive my soul at last.

2 Other refuge have I none;
  Hangs my helpless soul on thee;
Leave, ah, leave me not alone;
  Still support and comfort me:
All my trust on thee is stayed;
  All my hope from thee I bring;
Cover my defenceless head
  With the shadow of thy wing.

3 Thou, O Christ, art all I want;
  More than all in thee I find;
Raise the fallen, cheer the faint,
  Heal the sick, and lead the blind:

Thou of life the fountain art,
  Freely let me take of thee;
Spring thou up within my heart,
  Rise to all eternity.

68. *Trust in Christ.* C. M.

1 Jesus, the very thought of thee
   With sweetness fills my breast;
  But sweeter far thy face to see,
   And in thy presence rest.

2 Nor voice can sing, nor heart can frame,
   Nor can the memory find
  A sweeter sound than thy blest name,
   O Saviour of mankind!

3 Oh, hope of every contrite heart!
   Oh, joy of all the meek!
  To those who fall, how kind thou art!
   How good to those who seek!

4 But what to those who find? Ah! this
   Nor tongue nor pen can show,
  The love of Jesus, what it is,
   None but his loved ones know.

5 Jesus, our only joy be thou,
   As thou our prize wilt be;
  Jesus, be thou our glory now,
   And through eternity.

69. *The Mother of Christ.* 8s & 7s.

1 At the cross her station keeping,
  Stood the mournful mother weeping,
    Close to Jesus to the last:
  Through her heart, his sorrow sharing,
  All his bitter anguish bearing,
    Now at length the sword had passed.

2 Oh! how sad and sore distressed
  Was that mother, highly blest
    Of the sole-begotten One!
  Christ above in torment hangs,
  She beneath beholds the pangs
    Of her dying glorious Son.

3 Let me mingle tears with thee,
  Mourning him who mourned for me,
    All the days that I may live;
  By the cross with him to stay,
  There with thee to weep and pray,
    Is all I ask of Christ to give.

4 Christ, when thou shalt call me hence,
  Be thou only my defence,
    Be thy cross my victory;
  While my body here decays,
  May my soul thy goodness praise,
    Safe in paradise with thee.

THE HOLY SPIRIT.

70. *Veni Creator Spiritus.* C. M.

1 Spirit Divine! attend our prayer,
    And make our hearts thy home;
  Descend with all thy gracious power:
    Come, Holy Spirit, come!

2 Come as the light—to us reveal
    Our sinfulness and woe;
  And lead us in those paths of life
    Where all the righteous go.

3 Come as the fire, and purge our hearts
    Like sacrificial flame;

Let our whole soul an offering be
 To our Redeemer's name.

4 Come as the dew, and sweetly bless
 This consecrated hour;
May barrenness rejoice to own
 Thy fertilizing power.

5 Come as the wind with rushing sound,
 With Pentecostal grace,
And make the great salvation known
 Wide as the human race.

6 Spirit Divine, attend our prayer,
 And make our hearts thy home;
Descend with all thy glorious power:
 Come, Holy Spirit, come!

71. *The Spirit's Help.* 7s.

1 Holy Ghost! with light divine
Shine upon this heart of mine;
Chase the shades of night away;
Turn my darkness into day.

2 Holy Ghost! with power divine
Cleanse this guilty heart of mine;
Long hath sin, without control,
Held dominion o'er my soul.

3 Holy Ghost! with joy divine
Cheer this saddened heart of mine;
Bid my many woes depart;
Heal my wounded, bleeding heart.

4 Holy Ghost! thou, Lord Divine,
Dwell within this heart of mine;
Cast down every idol-throne—
Reign supreme, and reign alone.

72. *Ministry of the Spirit.* P. M.

1 Holy Spirit, Lord of light,
From thy clear celestial height,
  Thy pure beaming radiance give.
Come, thou Father of the poor,
Come with treasures which endure,
  Come, thou Light of all that live.

2 Thou, of all consolers best,
Visiting the troubled breast,
  Dost refreshing peace bestow;
Thou, in toil art comfort sweet,
Pleasant coolness in the heat,
  Solace in the midst of woe.

3 Light immortal, Light divine,
Visit thou these hearts of thine,
  And our inmost being fill;
If thou take thy grace away,
Nothing pure in man can stay,
  All his good is turned to ill.

4 Thou on those who evermore
Thee confess and thee adore,
  In thy sevenfold gifts descend;
Give them comfort when they die,
Give them life with thee on high,
  Give them joys which never end.

73. *The Witness of the Spirit.* C. M.

1 Come, Holy Ghost, our hearts inspire,
  Let us thine influence prove,
Source of the old prophetic fire,
  Fountain of life and love.

2 Come, Holy Ghost, for moved by thee,
    The prophets wrote and spoke;
Unlock the truth, thyself the key,
    Unseal the sacred book.

3 Expand thy wings, celestial Dove,
    Brood o'er our nature's night;
On our disordered spirits move,
    And let there now be light.

4 God through himself, we then shall know
    If thou within us shine;
And sound with all thy saints below,
    The depths of love divine.

74. *Descent of the Holy Spirit.* S. M.

1 From God, thou Holy Ghost,
    In this accepted hour,
As on the day of Pentecost,
    Descend in all thy power;
We meet with one accord
    In our appointed place,
And wait the promise of our Lord,
    The spirit of all grace.

2 Like a mighty rushing wind
    Upon the waves beneath,
Move with one impulse every mind,
    Our soul one feeling breathe;
The young, the old inspire
    With wisdom from above,
And give us hearts and tongues of fire,
    To pray, and praise, and love.

3 Spirit of light, explore,
    And chase our gloom away,
With lustre shining more and more
    Unto the perfect day.

Spirit of truth, be thou
　In life and death our guide;
O Spirit of adoption, now
　May we be sanctified.

75. *"The Comforter, which is the Holy Ghost."* 7s & 5s.

1 Holy Ghost, the Infinite!
Shine upon our nature's night
With thy blessed inward light,
　Comforter Divine!

2 We are sinful: cleanse us, Lord;
We are faint: thy strength afford;
Lost,—until by thee restored,
　Comforter Divine!

3 Like the dew, thy peace distil;
Guide, subdue our wayward will,
Things of Christ unfolding still,
　Comforter Divine!

4 In us, for us, intercede,
And, with voiceless groanings, plead
Our unutterable need,
　Comforter Divine!

5 In us "Abba, Father," cry—
Earnest of our bliss on high,
Seal of immortality,—
　Comforter Divine!

6 Search for us the depths of God;
Bear us up the starry road,
To the height of thine abode,
　Comforter Divine!

CHURCH SEASONS.

76. *Triumph of Christianity.* P. M.

1 Daughter of Zion, awake from thy sadness!
   Awake! for thy foes shall oppress thee no more;
Bright o'er thy hills dawns the Day-star of gladness;
   Arise! for the night of thy sorrow is o'er.

2 Strong were thy foes, but the arm that subdued them,
   And scattered their legions, was mightier far;
They fled like the chaff from the scourge that pursued
      them,
   Vain were their steeds and their chariots of war.

3 Daughter of Zion, the Power that hath saved thee,
   Extolled with the harp and the timbrel should be;
Shout! for the foe is destroyed that enslaved thee,
   The oppressor is vanquished, and Zion is free.

77. *The Birth of Christ.* P. M.

1   No war or battle's sound
    Was heard the world around,
  No hostile chiefs to furious combat ran;
    But peaceful was the night,
    In which the Prince of light,
  His reign of peace upon the earth began.

2   The shepherds on the lawn,
    Before the break of dawn,
  Sat silent, gazing on the starry sky;
    When, lo! a blaze of light
    Burst on their wondering sight,
  With fiery radiance kindling all on high;

3 And music, sweet and clear,
  Flowed on the listening ear,
Such as of old, the sons of morning sung:
  The gentle cherubim
  And shining seraphim
Welcomed their Prince with rapture on their tongue.

4 Hail! hail! auspicious morn!
  The Saviour Christ is born!
(Such was the immortal seraph's song sublime;)
  Glory to God in Heaven!
  On earth sweet peace be given,
Sweet peace and friendship to the end of time!

5 Oh, may the silver chime
  Sound through all coming time;
And let the bass of heaven's deep organ blow,
  To bless the Holy Child,
  Who came in winter wild,
To dwell with man in this cold world below.

78. *"Christ is born in Bethlehem."* 7s.

1 Hark! the herald angels sing,
  "Glory to the new-born King!
  Peace on earth, and mercy mild;
  God and sinners reconciled."

2 Joyful, all ye nations, rise;
  Join the triumphs of the skies;
  With the angelic hosts proclaim,
  "Christ is born in Bethlehem."

3 Mild he lays his glory by,
  Born that man, no more may die,
  Born to raise the sons of earth,
  Born to give them second birth.

4 Hail, the heaven-born Prince of Peace!
  Hail, the Sun of Righteousness!

Light and life to all he brings,
Risen with healing in his wings.

5 Let us then with angels sing,
"Glory to the new-born King!—
Peace on earth and mercy mild,
God and sinners reconciled!"

79.   *The Star of Bethlehem.*   L. M.

1 When marshalled on the nightly plain,
　The glittering host bestud the sky,
One star alone, of all the train,
　Can fix the sinner's wandering eye.

2 Hark! hark! to God the chorus breaks,
　From every host, from every gem;
But one alone, the Saviour, speaks:
　It is the Star of Bethlehem.

3 Once on the raging seas I rode:
　The storm was loud, the night was dark;
The ocean yawned, and rudely blowed
　The wind that tossed my foundering bark.

4 Deep horror then my vitals froze,
　Death-struck, I ceased the tide to stem,
When suddenly a star arose,
　It was the star of Bethlehem.

5 It was my guide, my light, my all,
　It bade my dark forebodings cease,
And through the storm, and danger's thrall,
　It led me to the port of peace.

6 Now safely moored, my perils o'er,
　I'll sing, first in night's diadem,
For ever and for evermore,
　The Star—the Star of Bethlehem!

80. *Christ the Way, the Truth, and the Life.* 10s.

1 O thou great Friend to all the sons of men,
  Who once appeared in humblest guise below,
Sin to rebuke, to break the captive's chain,
  And call thy brethren forth from want and woe.

2 We look to thee! thy truth is still the Light,
  Which guides the nations, groping on their way,
Stumbling and falling in disastrous night,
  Yet hoping ever for the perfect day,

3 Yes! thou art still the Life; thou art the Way
  The holiest know;—Light, Life, and Way of heaven!
And they who dearest hope, and deepest pray,
  Toil by the light, life, way, which thou hast given.

81. *Christ present in the Spirit.* 11s.

1 Oh, what though our feet may not tread where Christ trod,
Nor our ears hear the dashing of Galilee's flood,
Nor our eyes see the cross that he bowed him to bear,
Nor our knees press Gethsemane's garden of prayer!

2 Yet, Loved of the Father! thy spirit is near
To the meek and the lowly and the penitent here;
And the voice of thy love is the same, even now,
As at Bethany's tomb, or on Olivet's brow.

3 Oh, the Outward has gone, but in glory and power
The Spirit surviveth the things of an hour;
Unchanged, undecaying, its Pentecost flame
On the heart's secret altar is burning, the same.

82. *"Rock of Ages."* 7s.

1 Rock of Ages! cleft for me,
  Let me hide myself in thee!

  Let the water and the blood,
  From thy riven side that flowed,
  Be of sin the double cure—
  Cleanse me from its guilt and power.

2 Could my zeal no respite know,
  Could my tears for ever flow—
  All for sin could not atone:
  Thou must save, and thou alone!
  Nothing in my hand I bring,
  Simply to thy cross I cling.

3 While I draw this fleeting breath,
  When my eyelids close in death,
  When I soar to worlds unknown,
  See thee on thy judgment-throne,—
  Rock of Ages! cleft for me,
  Let me hide myself in thee!

83. *His final Entrance into Jerusalem.*

1 RIDE on, ride on in majesty!
  In lowly pomp ride on to die:
  O Christ! thy triumphs now begin
  O'er captive death and conquered sin.

2 Ride on, ride on in majesty!
  The wingèd squadrons of the sky
  Look down, with sad and wondering eyes,
  To see th' approaching sacrifice.

3 Ride on, ride on in majesty!
  Thy last and fiercest strife is nigh:
  The Father, on his sapphire throne,
  Expects his own anointed Son.

4 Ride on, ride on in majesty!
  In lowly pomp ride on to die:
  Bow thy meek head to mortal pain;
  Then take, O Lord, thy power, and reign!

84.   *" O sacred Head, now wounded!"*   7s & 6s.

1 O SACRED Head, now wounded!
    With grief and shame weighed down;
O sacred brow, surrounded
    With thorns, thine only crown!
Once on a throne of glory,
    Adorned with light divine,
Now all despised and gory,
    I joy to call thee mine.

2 On me, as thou art dying,
    Oh, turn thy pitying eye!
To thee for mercy crying,
    Before thy cross I lie.
Thine, thine the bitter passion,
    Thy pain is all for me;
Mine, mine the deep transgression,
    My sins are all on thee.

3 What language can I borrow
    To thank thee, dearest Friend,
For all this dying sorrow,
    Of all my woes the end?
Oh, can I leave thee ever?
    Then do not thou leave me:
Lord, let me never, never
    Outlive my love to thee.

4 Be near when I am dying;
    Then close beside me stand;
Let me, while faint and sighing,
    Lean calmly on thy hand:
These eyes, new faith receiving,
    From thine eye shall not move;
For he who dies believing,
    Dies safely in thy love.

85.   *A Communion Hymn.*   S. M.

1 Here in the broken bread,
   Here in the cup we take,
His body and his blood behold,
   Who suffered for our sake.

2 O thou who didst allow
   Thy Son to suffer thus,
Father, what more couldst thou have done
   Than thou hast done for us?

3 We are persuaded now
   That nothing can divide
Thy children from thy boundless love,
   Displayed in him who died;—

4 Who died to make us sure
   Of mercy, truth, and peace,
And from the power and pains of sin
   To bring a full release.

86.   *An Easter Hymn.*   P. M.

1 Awake, thou wintry earth—
   Fling off thy sadness!
Fair vernal flowers, laugh forth
   Your ancient gladness!
     Christ is risen!

2 Wave, woods, your blossoms all—
   Grim death is dead!
Ye weeping funeral trees,
   Lift up your head—
     Christ is risen!

3 Come, see! the graves are green;
   It is light—let's go

Where our loved ones rest
In hope below.
Christ is risen!

4 All is fresh and new,
Full of spring and light;
Wintry heart, why wear'st the hue
Of sleep and night?
Christ is risen!

5 Leave thy cares beneath,
Leave thy worldly love;
Begin the better life
With God above.
Christ is risen!

87. *Anthem for Easter Sunday.* 8s & 7s.

1 O God, my heart is fixed, 'tis bent
Its thankful tribute to present;
And with my heart my voice I'll raise
To thee, my God, in songs of praise.

2 Christ, the Lord, is risen to-day,
Sons of men and angels, cry;
Raise your joys and triumphs high;
Sing, ye heavens; and earth, reply.

3 The rising Lord forsakes the tomb,
Up to his Father's court he flies;
Cherubic legions guard him home,
And shout him welcome to the skies.

4 Love's redeeming work is done;
Fought the fight, the victory won;
Jesus' agony is o'er,
Darkness veils the earth no more.

5 Vain the stone, the watch, the seal,
　　Christ hath burst the bars of hell;
　Death in vain forbids him rise,
　　Christ hath opened paradise.
　　　　　　Hallelujah; Amen.

88. *The City of God.*

CHORUS.

　Shout the glad tidings, exultingly sing:
　　Jerusalem triumphs, Messiah is king!

1 Sion, the marvellous story be telling,
　　The Son of the highest, how lowly his birth!
　The brightest archangel in glory excelling,
　　He stoops to redeem thee, he reigns upon earth.
　　　Shout the glad tidings, &c.

2 Tell how he cometh; from nation to nation,
　　The heart-cheering news let the earth echo round;
　How free to the faithful he offers salvation,
　　How his people with joy everlasting are crowned.
　　　Shout the glad tidings, &c.

3 Mortals, your homage be gratefully bringing,
　　And sweet let the gladsome hosanna arise;
　Ye angels, the full hallelujah be singing:
　　One chorus resound through the earth and the skies.
　　　Shout the glad tidings, &c.

89. *The Coronation.* C. M.

1 All hail, the power of Jesus' name!
　　Let angels prostrate fall;
　Bring forth the royal diadem,
　　And crown him Lord of all!

2 Crown him, ye martyrs of our God,
　　Who from his altar call;

Extol the stem of Jesse's rod,
   And crown him Lord of all!

3 Ye chosen seed of Israel's race,
   A remnant weak and small,
Hail him who saves you by his grace,
   And crown him Lord of all!

4 Ye Gentile sinners, ne'er forget
   The wormwood and the gall;
Go, spread your trophies at his feet,
   And crown him Lord of all!

5 Let every kindred, every tribe,
   On this terrestrial ball,
To him all majesty ascribe,
   And crown him Lord of all!

6 Oh, that, with yonder sacred throng,
   We at his feet may fall!
We'll join the everlasting song,
   And crown him Lord of all!

90.   "*Strike the cymbal.*"   8s & 7s.

1 STRIKE the cymbal, roll the timbrel,
   Let the trump of triumph sound;
Joyous singing, tributes bringing,
   Th' isles exult, and seas resound.

2 Lo! he's risen from death's dark prison,
   Rays divine his eyes relume;
Judah's Lion, King of Zion,
   Lord o'er death, hath fled the tomb.

3 Judah's Lion, King of Zion,
   Lord o'er death, hath fled the tomb;
   Alleluia! alleluia!
Mortals, strike your tuneful lyres—
Holy mirth the day inspires.

4 What are nations—what their stations?—
   God in Christ is Lord of hosts,
God of thunder, Lord of wonder:
   Vain are mortals, vain their boasts.

5 What are Jewry's monarchs now!
   Low before Emanuel bow,
Holy Son of God supreme,
   Mortal, mortals to redeem.
     Praise him, praise him,
     Exulting nations, praise;
     Praise him, praise him,
     Exulting nations, praise.
     Hosanna, hosanna, hosanna!

91.   *Glorying in the Cross.*   8s & 7s.

1 In the cross of Christ we glory,
   Towering o'er the wrecks of time;
All the light of sacred story
   Gathers round its head sublime.

2 When the woes of life o'ertake us,
   Hopes deceive, and fears annoy;
Never shall the cross forsake us,
   Lo! it glows with peace and joy!

3 When the sun of bliss is beaming
   Light and love upon our way;
From the cross the radiance streaming
   Adds more lustre to the day.

4 Bane and blessing, pain and pleasure,
   By the cross are sanctified;
Peace is there that knows no measure,
   Joys that through all time abide.

5 In the cross of Christ we glory,
  Towering o'er the wrecks of time;
 All the light of sacred story
  Gathers round its head sublime.

92.   *Easter Hymn.*   P. M.

1 LIFT your glad voices in triumph on high,
  For Jesus hath risen, and man cannot die.
 Vain were the terrors that gathered around him,
  And short the dominion of death and the grave;
 He burst from the fetters of darkness that bound him,
  Resplendent in glory, to live and to save.
 Loud was the chorus of angels on high,—
 "The Saviour hath risen, and man shall not die."

2 Glory to God, in full anthems of joy;
  The being he gave us death cannot destroy.
 Sad were the life we must part with to-morrow,
  If tears were our birthright, and death were our end:
 But Jesus hath cheered the dark valley of sorrow,
  And bade us, immortal, to heaven ascend.
 Lift, then, your voices in triumph on high,
 For Jesus hath risen, and man shall not die.

93.   *Christ is risen.*   7s.

1 ANGEL, roll the stone away!
 Death, give up thy mighty prey!
 See, he rises from the tomb,
 Glowing in immortal bloom.

2 Shout, ye saints, in rapturous song;
 Let the notes be sweet and strong;
 Hail the Son of God, this morn,
 From his sepulchre new born!

3 Christians, dry your flowing tears;
  Calm those unbelieving fears;
  Doubt no more his power to save;
  See his own deserted grave!

4 Powers of heaven, seraphic fires,
  Sing, and sweep your sounding lyres;
  Sons of men, in joyful strain
  Hail your mighty Saviour's reign!

5 Every note with rapture swell,
  And the Saviour's triumph tell;
  Where, O Death, is now thy sting?
  Where thy terrors, vanquished king?

94. *The Ascension.* C. M.

1 THE Apostles on the mountain stand—
  The mystic mount—in Holy Land;
  They, with the blessed Mother, see
  Jesus ascend in majesty.

2 The angels say to the eleven,—
  "Why stand ye gazing into heaven?
  This is the Saviour—this is he!
  Jesus hath triumphed gloriously!"

3 May our affections thither tend,
  And thither constantly ascend,
  Where, seated on the Father's throne,
  Thee reigning in the heavens we own!

4 Be thou our present joy, O Lord,
  Who wilt be ever sure reward;
  And as the countless ages flee,
  May all our glory be in Thee!

95.   *Pentecost.*   C. M.

1 When first the Spirit of our God
    Came down his flock to find,
  A voice from heaven was heard abroad,
    A rushing mighty wind.

2 Nor doth the outward ear alone
    At that high warning start;
  Conscience gives back the appalling tone;
    'Tis echoed in the heart.

3 It fills the church of God; it fills
    The sinful world around;
  Only in stubborn hearts and wills
    No place for it is found.

4 To other strains such souls are set;
    A giddy whirl of sin
  Fills ear and brain, and will not let
    Heaven's harmonies come in.

5 Come, Lord, come Wisdom, Love, and Power,
    Open our ears to hear;
  Let us not miss the accepted hour;
    Save, Lord, by love or fear.

96.   *Whitsunday.*   7s.

1 Holy Spirit; Love Divine!
    Let thy light within me shine;
  Breathe thyself into my breast:
    Earnest of immortal rest.

2 Let me never from thee stray,
    Keep me in the narrow way:
  Keep me thine, for ever thine;
    Let thy love and joy be mine.

97. *Baptism of a Child.* S. M.

1 To thee, O God in heaven,
　This little one we bring,
Giving to thee what thou hast given,
　Our dearest offering.

2 Into a world of toil
　These little feet will roam,
Where sin its purity may soil,
　Where care and grief may come.

3 Oh, then, let thy pure love,
　With influence serene,
Come down, like water, from above,
　To comfort and make clean!

98. *Baptism of Children.* S. M.

1 To Him who children blest,
　And suffered them to come,
To Him who took them to his breast,
　We bring these children home.

2 To thee, O God, whose face
　Their spirits still behold,
We bring them, praying that thy grace
　May keep, thine arms enfold.

3 And as this water falls
　On each unconscious brow,
Thy Holy Spirit grant, O Lord,
　To keep them pure as now!

99. *Baptism of Infants.* 8s & 7s.

1 SAVIOUR, who thy flock art feeding,
　With the shepherd's kindest care,
All the feeble gently leading,
　While the lambs thy bosom share;

2 Now, *these* little *ones* receiving,
    Fold *them* in thy gracious arm;
There, we know, thy word believing,
    Only there, secure from harm.

3 Never, from thy pasture roving,
    Let *them* be the Lion's prey;
Let thy tenderness, so loving,
    Keep *them* all life's dangerous way:

4 Then, within thy fold eternal,
    Let *them* find a resting-place;
Feed in pastures ever vernal,
    Drink the rivers of thy grace.

100.   *Christ our Life.*   7s & 6s.

1 O BREAD to pilgrims given,
    O food that angels eat,
O manna sent from heaven,
    For heaven-born natures meet!
Give us, for thee long pining,
    To eat till richly filled;
Till, earth's delights resigning,
    Our every wish is stilled!

2 O water, life-bestowing,
    From out the Saviour's heart,
A fountain purely flowing,
    A fount of love thou art!
Oh, let us, freely tasting,
    Our burning thirst assuage!
Thy sweetness, never wasting,
    Avails from age to age.

3 Jesus, this feast receiving,
    We thee unseen adore;
Thy faithful word believing,
    We take—and doubt no more;

Give us, thou true and loving,
  On earth to live in thee;
Then, death the veil removing,
  Thy glorious face to see!

101. *One in Christ.*

1 Planted in Christ, the living Vine,
  This day, with one accord,
Ourselves, with humble faith and joy,
  We yield to thee, O Lord!

2 Joined in one body may we be;
  One inward life partake;
One be our heart, one heavenly hope
  In every bosom wake.

3 In prayer, in effort, tears, and toils,
  One Wisdom be our guide;
Taught by one Spirit from above,
  In thee may we abide.

4 Then, when among the saints in light
  Our joyful spirits shine,
Shall anthems of immortal praise,
  O Lamb of God, be thine.

102. *One in Christ.*

1 A holy air is breathing round,
  A fragrance from above;
Be every soul from sense unbound,
  Be every spirit love.

2 O God, unite us heart to heart,
  In sympathy divine,
That we be never drawn apart,
  And love not thee nor thine:

3 But, by the cross of Jesus taught,
  And all thy gracious word,
Be nearer to each other brought,
  And nearer to the Lord.

103.   *"Thy people shall be my people, and thy*   7s.
        God my God."

1 People of the living God,
  I have sought the world around,
Paths of sin and sorrow trod,
  Peace and comfort nowhere found.

2 Now to you my spirit turns—
  Turns, a fugitive unblest;
Brethren! where your altar burns,
  Oh, receive me into rest!

3 Lonely I no longer roam,
  Like the cloud, the wind, the wave;
Where you dwell shall be my home,
  Where you die shall be my grave;

4 Mine the God whom you adore,
  Your Redeemer shall be mine;
Earth can fill my soul no more,
  Every idol I resign.

104.   *Communion Hymn.*   7s.

1 While we here remember thee,
  Who wast for our ransom slain,
Let thy love, thy purity,
  Saviour, in our souls remain.

2 Father, while we break this bread,
  And thy Christ remember thus,
Make us one with him, our Head,
  Thou in him, and he in us.

3 While to lips with praise that glow,
   This communion cup we press,
Holy Father, help us grow
   More like him we here confess.

4 Reconcile us by thy Son,
   In whose name on thee we call;
Make us perfect, all in one—
   We in him, and thou in all.

105.   *Ordination Hymn.*   7s.

1 Mighty One, before whose face
   Wisdom had her glorious seat,
When the orbs that people space
   Sprang to birth beneath thy feet!

2 Source of truth, whose rays alone
   Light the mighty world of mind!
God of love, who from thy throne
   Kindly watchest all mankind!

3 Shed, on those who in thy name
   Teach the way of truth and right,
Shed that love's undying flame,
   Shed that wisdom's guiding light.

106.   "*Behold, the tabernacle of God is with men.*"   7s.

1 Hark! the song of Jubilee!
   Loud as mighty thunders' roar,
Or the fulness of the sea,
   When it breaks upon the shore.
Hallelujah! for the Lord
   God Omnipotent shall reign:
Hallelujah! let the word
   Echo round the earth and main!

2 Hallelujah! hark, the sound,
   From the centre to the skies,
Wakes, above, beneath, around,
   All creation's harmonies
See! Jehovah's banner's furled,
   Sheathed his sword—he speaks, 'tis done,
And the kingdoms of this world
   Are the kingdoms of his Son.

3 He shall reign from pole to pole,
   With illimitable sway;
He shall reign when, like a scroll,
   Yonder heavens have passed away.
Then the end—beneath his rod
   Man's last enemy shall fall.
Hallelujah! Christ in God,
   God in Christ is all in all!

THE CHRISTIAN LIFE.

107.   *Invocation.*   7s.

1 SOVEREIGN and transforming grace!
   We invoke thy quickening power;
Reign, the spirit of this place,
   Bless the purpose of this hour.

2 Holy and creative Light,
   We invoke thy kindling ray;
Dawn upon our spirits' night,
   Turn our darkness into day.

3 To the anxious soul impart
   Hope all other hopes above;
Stir the dull and hardened heart
   With a longing and a love.

4 Give the struggling peace for strife,
    Give the doubting light for gloom,
Speed the living into life,
    Warn the dying of their doom.

5 Work in all; in all renew,
    Day by day, the life divine;
All our wills to thee subdue,
    All our hearts to thee incline.

108.   *Let there be Light!*

1 Thou whose almighty word
  Chaos and darkness heard,
    And took their flight!
Hear us, we humbly pray,
And where the gospel day
Sheds not its glorious ray,
    Let there be light!

2 Thou who didst come to bring,
  On thy redeeming wing,
    Healing and sight,
Health to the sick in mind,
Light to the inly blind,
Oh, now, to all mankind
    Let there be light!

3 Descend thou from above,
  Spirit of truth and love,
    Speed on thy flight!
Move o'er the waters' face,
Spirit of hope and grace,
And in earth's darkest place
    Let there be light!

109.   *Longing for Christ.*   8s & 6s.

1 Jesus, the strength of angels strong,
　Thy name excels the sweetest song,
　Dropping like nectar from the tongue—
　　Like nectar in the heart.

2 Wherever I may chance to be,
　Thee first my heart desires to see;
　How glad when I discover thee,
　　How blest when I retain!

3 Beyond all treasures is thy grace;
　Oh! when wilt thou thy steps retrace,
　And satisfy me with thy face,
　　And make me wholly glad?

4 Then come, oh, come, thou perfect King
　Of boundless glory, boundless spring!
　Arise, and fullest daylight bring,
　　Jesus, expected long!

5 Fountain of mercy and of love,
　Sun of the Fatherland above,
　The cloud of sadness far remove,
　　The light of glory give!

110.   *Oh, move me!*   L. M.

1 God namèd Love, whose fount thou art,
　　Thy crownless church before thee stands,
　With too much hating in her heart,
　　With too much striving in her hands.

2 Yet, Lord, thy wrongèd love fulfil!
　　Thy church, though fallen, before thee stands—
　Behold, the voice is Jacob's still,
　　Albeit the hands are Esau's hands!

3 Oh, move us—thou hast power to move—
 One in the one Beloved to be!
Teach us the heights and depths of love,
 Give thine, that we may love like thee!

111.   *"I will arise and go unto my father."*   L. M.

1 To thine eternal arms, O God,
 Take us, thine erring children, in;
From dangerous paths too boldly trod,
 From wandering thoughts and dreams of sin.

2 Those arms were round our childhood's ways,
 A guard through helpless years to be;
Oh, leave not our maturer days;
 We still are helpless without thee.

3 We trusted pride, and hope, and strength;
 Our strength proved false, our pride was vain,
Our dreams have faded all at length;
 We come to thee, O Lord, again.

4 A guide to trembling steps yet be;
 Give us of thine eternal powers;
So shall our paths all lead to thee,
 And life smile on like childhood's hours.

112.   *True Strength.*   S. M.

1 "When I am weak, I'm strong,"
 The great Apostle cried;
What did not to the earth belong,
 The might of heaven supplied.

2 "When I am weak, I'm strong,"
 Each Christian heart repeats,
To tune its feeblest breath to song,
 And fire its languid beats.

3 O holy Strength! whose ground
 Is in the heavenly land;
Supporting help alone is found
 In God's immortal hand.

4 O Blessèd! that appears
 When fleshly aids are spent,
And girds the mind, when most it fears,
 With trust and sweet content.

113.   *Uses of Affliction.*   8s & 7s.

1 As the harp-strings only render
 All their treasures of sweet sound,
All their music, glad or tender,
 Firmly struck and tightly bound:

2 So the hearts of Christians owe
 Each its deepest, sweetest strain,
To the pressure firm of woe,
 And the tension tight of pain.

3 Spices crushed their pungence yield;
 Trodden scents their sweets respire;
Would you have its strength revealed,
 Cast the incense on the fire.

4 Thus the crushed and broken frame
 Oft doth sweetest graces yield;
And through suffering, toil, and shame,
 Heavenly incense is distilled!

114.   *Comfort in Sorrow.*   7s & 6s.

1 Up! up! the day is breaking,
 Say to thy cares, Good-night!
Thy troubles from thee shaking,
 Like dreams in day's fresh light.

Thou wearest not the crown,
   Nor the best course canst tell;
God sitteth on the throne,
   He doeth all things well!

2 Trust him to govern, then!
   No king can rule like him;
How wilt thou wonder, when
   Thine eyes no more are dim;
To see these paths which vex thee,
   How wise they were, and meet!
The works which now perplex thee,
   How beautiful complete!

3 Faithful the love thou sharest,
   All, all is well with thee;
The crown from hence thou bearest
   With shouts of victory.
In thy right hand, to-morrow
   Thy God shall place the palms;
To him who chased thy sorrow,
   How glad will be thy psalms!

115. *Midnight Hymn.* P. M.

1 At midnight bursts the cry,
   So saith the Evangelist,
"Arise! the Bridegroom draweth nigh,
   The King of heaven, the Christ!"

2 The foolish virgins sleep,
   They seek for light too late;
In vain they knock, and call, and weep,
   Closed is the palace gate.

3 Let us keep steadfast guard,
   With lighted hearts all night;
That when He comes we stand prepared,
   And meet him with delight.

4 Meet for thy realm in heaven,
  Make us, O holy King!
That through the ages it be given
  To us thy praise to sing.

116. *Cry of the Afflicted.* 6s & 4s.

1 Lowly and solemn be
  Thy children's cry to thee,
    Father divine!
  A hymn of suppliant breath,
  Owning that life and death
    Alike are thine.

2 O Father, in that hour
  When earth all succoring power
    Shall disavow—
  When spear, and shield, and crown
  In faintness are cast down,—
    Sustain us, Thou!

3 By him who bowed to take
  The death-cup for our sake,
    The thorn, the rod,—
  From whom the last dismay
  Was not to pass away,—
    Aid us, O God!

4 Tremblers beside the grave,
  We call on thee to save,
    Father divine!
  Hear, hear our suppliant breath;
  Keep us, in life or death,
    Thine, only thine!

117. *"Come unto me, all ye that labor."* L. M.

1 Peace, troubled soul, whose plaintive moan
  Hath taught each scene the notes of woe;

Cease thy complaint, suppress thy groan,
    And let thy tears forget to flow:
Behold, the precious balm is found,
To lull thy pain, to heal thy wound.

2 Come, freely come, by sin oppressed,
    On Jesus cast thy weighty load,
In him thy refuge find, thy rest,
    Safe in the mercy of thy God:
Thy God's thy Saviour—glorious word!
Oh, hear, believe, and bless the Lord!

118.   *"Out of the depths have I cried unto thee."*   S. M.

1 Out of the depths of woe,
    To thee, O Lord! I cry;
Darkness surrounds me, yet I know
    That thou art ever nigh.

2 I cast my hopes on thee,
    Thou canst, thou wilt forgive;
If thou shouldst mark iniquity,
    Who in thy sight could live?

3 I wait for thee; I wait,
    Confessing all my sin;
Lord! I am knocking at thy gate,
    Open, and take me in.

4 Glory to God above!
    The waters soon will cease;
For lo! the swift-returning dove
    Brings home the pledge of peace.

5 Though storms his face obscure,
    And dangers threaten loud,
Jehovah's covenant is sure,
    His bow is in the cloud!

119.   *No rest but in God.*   6s.

1 My soul doth long for thee
    To dwell within my breast;
 Unworthy though I be
    Of so divine a Guest!

2 Of so divine a Guest
    Unworthy though I be,
 Yet hath my heart no rest
    Until it come to thee!

3 Until it come to thee,
    In vain I look around;
 In all that I can see,
    No rest is to be found!

4 No rest is to be found,
    But in thy bleeding love;
 Oh, let my wish be crowned,
    And send it from above!

120.   *"The Greatest of these is Charity."*   8s & 7s.

1 Meek and lowly, pure and holy,
    Chief among the blessèd three,
 Turning sadness into gladness,
    Heaven-born art thou, Charity!

2 Pity dwelleth in thy bosom,
    Kindness reigneth o'er thy heart;
 Gentle thoughts alone can sway thee—
    Censure hath in thee no part.

3 Hoping ever, failing never,
    Though deceived, believing still;
 Long abiding, all confiding,
    To thy heavenly Father's will.

4 Never weary of well-doing,
   Never fearful of the end;
Claiming all mankind as brothers,
   Thou dost all alike befriend.

5 Meek and lowly, pure and holy,
   Chief among the blessèd three,
Turning sadness into gladness,
   Heaven-born art thou, Charity!

121. *Prayer for Help at all Times.* L. M.

1 Is there a lone and dreary hour,
When worldly pleasures lose their power?
My Father! let me turn to thee,
And set each thought of darkness free.

2 Is there a time of racking grief,
Which scorns the prospect of relief?
My Father! break the cheerless gloom,
And bid my heart its calm resume.

3 Is there an hour of peace and joy,
When hope is all my soul's employ?
My Father! still my hopes will roam,
Until they rest with thee, their home.

4 The noontide blaze, the midnight scene,
The dawn, or twilight's sweet serene,
The glow of health, the dying hour,
Shall own my Father's grace and power.

122. *"Come to the Ark."* C. M.

1 COME to the ark, come to the ark,
   To Jesus come away,
The pestilence walks forth by night,
   The arrow flies by day.

2 Come to the ark: the waters rise,
    The seas their billows rear,
  While darkness gathers o'er the skies,
    Behold a refuge near!

3 Come to the ark, all, all that weep
    Beneath the sense of sin;
  Without, deep calleth unto deep,
    But all is peace within.

4 Come to the ark, ere yet the flood
    Your lingering steps oppose;
  Come, for the door which open stood
    Is now about to close.

123.   *"I will love thee, O Lord, my strength."*   10s & 6s.

1 I LOVE my God, but with no love of mine,
      For I have none to give;
  I love thee, Lord, but all the love is thine,
      For by thy life I live:
  I am as nothing, and rejoice to be
  Emptied, and lost, and swallowed up in thee.

2 Thou, Lord, alone art all thy children need,
      And there is none beside;
  From thee the streams of blessedness proceed,
      In thee the blest abide,—
  Fountain of life and all-abounding grace,
  Our Source, our Centre, and our Dwelling-place.

124.   *"Faint, yet pursuing."*   11s.

1 THOUGH faint, yet pursuing, we go on our way,
  The Lord is our Leader, his word is our stay;
  Though suffering, and sorrow, and trial be near,
  The Lord is our refuge, and whom can we fear!

2 He raiseth the fallen, he cheereth the faint;
　The weak and oppressed—he will hear their complaint;
　The way may be weary, and thorny the road,
　But how can we falter? our help is in God!

3 And to his green pastures our footsteps he leads;
　His flock in the desert how kindly he feeds!
　The lambs in his bosom he tenderly bears,
　And brings back the wanderers all safe from the snares.

4 Though clouds may surround us, our God is our light;
　Though storms rage around us, our God is our might;
　So faint, yet pursuing, still onward we come,
　The Lord is our Leader, and heaven is our home!

125. *"Oh, happy day, that fixed my choice."* L. M.

1 Oh, happy day, that fixed my choice
　　On thee, my Saviour, and my God!
　Well may this glowing heart rejoice,
　　And tell its raptures all abroad.

2 Oh, happy bond, that seals my vows
　　To him who merits all my love!
　Let cheerful anthems fill his house,
　　While to that sacred shrine I move.

3 'Tis done, the great transaction's done;
　　I am my Lord's, and he is mine;
　He drew me, and I followed on,
　　Charmed to confess the voice divine.

4 Now, rest, my long-divided heart!
　　Fixed on this blissful centre, rest;
　With ashes who would grudge to part,
　　When called on angels' bread to feast.

5 High Heaven, that heard the solemn vow,
　　That vow renewed shall daily hear,

Till in life's latest hour I bow,
And bless in death a bond so dear.

126. *Mary.* P. M.

1 Her eyes are homes of silent prayer,
 Nor other thought her mind admits,
 But—he was dead, and there he sits,
And He that brought him back, is there.

2 Then one deep love doth supersede
 All other, when her ardent gaze
 Roves from the living brother's face,
And rests upon the Life indeed.

3 All subtle thought, all curious fears,
 Borne down by gladness so complete,
 She bows, she bathes the Saviour's feet
With costly spikenard and with tears.

4 Thrice blest whose lives are faithful prayers,
 Whose loves in higher love endure;
 What souls possess themselves so pure,
Or is there blessedness like theirs?

127. *Joy over the Returning Prodigal.* S. M.

1 Hark! through the courts of heaven
  Angelic voices sound,
 He that was dead now lives again,
  He that was lost is found.

2 God of unfailing grace,
  Send down thy Spirit now;
 Oh, raise the lowly soul to hope,
  And make the lofty bow.

3 In countries far from home,
  On earthly husks who feed,

Back to their Father's house, O Lord,
    Their wandering footsteps lead.

4 Then at each soul's return,
    The heavenly harp shall sound;
He that was dead now lives again,
    He that was lost is found!

128.   "*Renew a right spirit within me.*"   7s & 6s.

1 GREAT Author of my being,
    I am consumed with care;
The ills of thy decreeing,
    Enable me to bear:
The spirit of contrition,
    Oh, may I now receive;
For all my soul's ambition
    Is worthily to grieve!

2 The grief beyond expressing,
    To me, O Lord, impart;
I ask this only blessing—
    An humble, broken heart:
The justice of thy sentence
    With meekest awe to own;
And spend, in deep repentance,
    My last, expiring groan.

3 In that decisive hour,
    When pain, with life, shall end,
Then, O thou God of power,
    Thou God of love, attend!
And bear, oh, bear my burden,
    And help my last distress;
And give me back my pardon,
    And bid me die in peace!

THE CHRISTIAN LIFE.

129. *"Fear not, little flock."* 7s & 6s.

1 In heavenly love abiding,
  No change my heart shall fear,
And safe is such confiding,
  For nothing changes here:
The storm may roar without me,
  My heart may low be laid,
But God is round about me,
  And can I be dismayed?

2 Wherever he may guide me,
  No want shall turn me back;
My Shepherd is beside me,
  And nothing can I lack:
His wisdom ever waketh,
  His sight is never dim:
He knows the way he taketh,
  And I will walk with him.

3 Green pastures are before me,
  Which yet I have not seen;
Bright skies will soon be o'er me,
  Where darkest clouds have been:
My hope I cannot measure,
  My path to life is free,
My Saviour has my treasure,
  And he will walk with me.

130. *"It is well."* 8s & 4s.

1 Through the love of God our Saviour,
  All will be well:
Free and changeless is his favor;
  All, all is well:

Precious is the blood that healed us;
Perfect is the grace that sealed us;
Strong the hand stretched out to shield us;
    All must be well.

2 Though we pass through tribulation,
    All will be well;
Ours is such a full salvation;
    All, all is well:
Happy, still in God confiding,
Fruitful, if in Christ abiding,
Holy, through the Spirit's guiding,
    All must be well.

3 We expect a bright to-morrow;
    All will be well:
Faith can sing through days of sorrow,
    All, all is well:
On our Father's love relying,
Jesus every need supplying,
Or in living, or in dying,
    All must be well.

131.   *" Come, thou Fount of every blessing."*   8s & 7s.

1 Come, thou Fount of every blessing,
    Tune my heart to sing thy grace;
Streams of mercy, never ceasing,
    Call for songs of loudest praise.

2 Teach me some melodious measure,
    Sung by flaming tongues above;
Oh, the vast, the boundless treasure
    Of thy free, unchanging love!

3 Jesus sought me when a stranger,
    Wandering from the fold of God;
He, to rescue me from danger,
    Interposed his precious blood.

4 Oh, to grace how great a debtor
 Daily I'm constrained to be!
Let thy goodness, like a fetter,
 Bind my wandering heart to thee.

5 Prone to wander, Lord, I feel it;
 Prone to leave the God I love:
Here's my heart; oh, take and seal it—
 Seal it for thy courts above!

132.   *The Inner Calm.*   C. M.

1 Calm me, my God, and keep me calm:
 Let thine outstretchèd wing
Be like the shade of Elim's palm
 Beside her desert spring.

2 Yes, keep me calm, though loud and rude
 The sounds my ear that greet,—
Calm in the closet's solitude,
 Calm in the bustling street,—

3 Calm in the hour of buoyant health,
 Calm in the hour of pain,
Calm in my poverty or wealth,
 Calm in my loss or gain,—

4 Calm in the sufferance of wrong,
 Like Him who bore my shame,
Calm mid the threatening, taunting throng,
 Who hate thy holy name.

5 Calm me, my God, and keep me calm,
 Soft resting on thy breast;
Soothe me with holy hymn and psalm,
 And bid my spirit rest.

THE CHRISTIAN LIFE.

133.   "*I press toward the mark.*"   10s, 11s & 12s.

1 Breast the wave, Christian, when it is strongest;
Watch for day, Christian, when night is longest;
Onward and onward still be thine endeavor;
The rest that remaineth, endureth for ever.

2 Fight the fight, Christian, Jesus is o'er thee;
Run the race, Christian, heaven is before thee;
He who hath promisèd faltereth never;
Oh, trust in the love that endureth for ever.

3 Lift the eye, Christian, just as it closeth;
Raise the heart, Christian, ere it reposeth:
Nothing thy soul from the Saviour shall sever;
Soon shalt thou mount upward to praise him for ever.

134.   "*Oh, for a lowly, contrite heart!*"   C. M.

1 Oh for a heart to praise my God!
   A heart from sin set free;
A heart that's sprinkled with the blood
   So freely shed for me;—

2 A heart resigned, submissive, meek,
   My dear Redeemer's throne;
Where only Christ is heard to speak,
   Where Jesus reigns alone!

3 Oh, for a lowly, contrite heart,
   Believing, true, and clean;
Which neither life nor death can part
   From him that dwells within!

4 Thy nature, gracious Lord, impart;
   Come quickly from above;
Write thy new name upon my heart—
   Thy new, best name of Love.

135.   *Stabat mater.*   P. M.

1 Jews were wrought to cruel madness,
Christians fled in fear and sadness,
   Mary stood the cross beside.

2 At its foot her foot she planted,
By the dreadful scene undaunted,
   Till the gentle sufferer died.

3 Poets oft have sung her story;
Painters decked her brow with glory;
   Priests her name have deified;

4 But no worship, song, or glory,
Touches like that simple story,—
   "Mary stood the cross beside."

5 And when under fierce oppression
Goodness suffers like transgression,
   Christ again is crucified.

6 But if love be there, true-hearted,
By no grief or terror parted,
   Mary stands the cross beside.

136.   *Thanks for all Saints.*   S. M.

1 For all thy saints, O God,
   Who strove in Christ to live,
Who followed him, obeyed, adored,
   Our grateful hymn receive.

2 For all thy saints, O God,
   Accept our thankful cry,
Who counted Christ their great reward,
   And yearned for him to die.

3 They all, in life and death,
   With him, their Lord, in view,
Learned from thy Holy Spirit's breath
   To suffer and to do.

4 For this, thy Name we bless,
   And humbly pray that we
May follow them in holiness,
   And live and die in thee.

137.   *"Is it such a fast that I have chosen?"*   C. M.

1 Do I delight in sorrow's dress
   (Saith he who reigns above);
The hanging head and rueful look,
   Will they attract my love?

2 Let such as feel oppression's load
   Thy tender pity share;
And let the helpless, homeless poor
   Be thy peculiar care.

3 Go, bid the hungry orphan be
   With thy abundance blest;
Invite the wanderer to thy gate,
   And spread the couch of rest.

4 Let him who pines with piercing cold
   By thee be warmed and clad;
Be thine the blissful task to make
   The downcast mourner glad.

5 Then, bright as morning shall come forth,
   In peace and joy, thy days;
And glory from the Lord above
   Shall shine on all thy ways.

THE CHRISTIAN LIFE.

138.   *"All the trees of the field shall clap their hands."*   7s & 6s.

1 When shall the voice of singing
   Flow joyfully along?
When hill and valley, ringing
   With one triumphant song,
Proclaim the contest ended,
   And him who once was slain,
Again to earth descended,
   In righteousness to reign?

2 Then from the craggy mountains
   The sacred shout shall fly;
And shady vales and fountains
   Shall echo the reply:
High tower and lowly dwelling
   Shall send the hymn around,
All hallelujah swelling
   In one eternal sound!

139.   *The Mother's Hymn.*   L. M.

1 Lord, who ordainest for mankind,
   Benignant toils and tender cares,
We thank thee for the ties that bind
   The mother to the child she bears.

2 We thank thee for the hopes that rise
   Within her heart, as, day by day,
The dawning soul from those young eyes
   Looks with a clearer, steadier ray.

3 And, grateful for the blessing given,
   With that dear infant on her knee,
She trains the eye to look to heaven,
   The voice to lisp a prayer to thee.

4 Such thanks the blessed Mary gave,
    When from her lap the Holy Child,
Sent from above to seek and save
    The lost of earth, looked up and smiled.

5 All-gracious! grant to those who bear
    A mother's charge, the strength and light
To guide the feet that own their care
    In ways of Love and Truth and Right.

140. *Children and Congregation.*   6s & 8s.

CHILDREN.

1 Come let our voices join
    In one glad song of praise;
To God, the God of love,
    Our grateful hearts we raise:

CONGREGATION.

To God alone your praise belongs;
His love demands your earliest songs.

CHILDREN.

2 Now we are taught to read
    The book of life divine;
Where our Redeemer's love,
    And brightest glories shine:

CONGREGATION.

To God alone the praise is due,
Who sends his word to us and you.

CHILDREN.

3 Within these hallowed walls,
    Our wandering feet are brought;
Where prayer and praise ascend,
    And heavenly truths are taught:

CONGREGATION.

To God alone your offerings bring;
Here in his church his praises sing.

CHILDREN.

4 For blessings such as these,
　　Our gratitude receive;
　Lord, here accept our hearts,
　　'Tis all that we can give:

CONGREGATION.

Great God, accept their infant songs;
To thee alone their praise belongs.

BOTH.

5 Lord, bid this work of love
　　Be crowned with meet success;
　May thousands yet unborn
　　This institution bless:
　Thus shall the praise resound to thee,
　Now, and through all eternity.

141.　　　　*The true use of Music.*　　　8s & 7s.

1 Who hath a right like us to sing—
　　Us whom his mercy raises?
　Merry our hearts, for Christ is king;
　　Cheerful are all our faces.
　Who of his love doth once partake,
　　He evermore rejoices;
　Melody in all our hearts we make,
　　Melody with our voices.

2 He that a sprinkled conscience hath—
　　He that in God is merry,
　Let him sing psalms, the Spirit saith,
　　Joyful, and never weary;

Offer the sacrifice of praise,
  Hearty and never ceasing;
Spiritual songs and anthems raise,
  Honor, and thanks, and blessing.

3 Then let us in his praises join,
    Triumph in his salvation;
  Glory ascribe to love divine,
    Worship and adoration.
  Heaven already is begun—
    Opened in each believer;
  Only believe, and still sing on,
    Heaven is ours for ever.

IMMORTALITY.

142. *" Abide with us, for it is toward evening."* 8s & 7s.

1 TARRY with me, O my Saviour!
    For the day is passing by;
  See! the shades of evening gather,
    And the night is drawing nigh.

2 Deeper, deeper grow the shadows,
    Paler now the glowing west,
  Swift the night of death advances;
    Shall it be the night of rest?

3 Feeble, trembling, fainting, dying,
    Lord, I cast myself on thee;
  Tarry with me through the darkness;
    While I sleep, still watch by me.

4 Tarry with me, O my Saviour!
    Lay my head upon thy breast
  Till the morning; then awake me—
    Morning of eternal rest!

143. *"Weep not: she is not dead, but sleepeth."* 8s & 7s.

1 Sister, thou wast mild and lovely,
 Gentle as the summer breeze;
Pleasant as the air of evening,
 When it floats among the trees.

2 Peaceful be thy silent slumber—
 Peaceful in the grave so low:
Thou no more wilt join our number;
 Thou no more our songs shalt know

3 Dearest sister, thou hast left us;
 Here thy loss we deeply feel;
But 'tis God that hath bereft us,
 He can all our sorrows heal.

4 Yet again we hope to meet thee,
 When the day of life is fled;
Then in heaven with joy to greet thee,
 Where no farewell tear is shed!

144. *Requiem of Heroes.*

1 How sleep the brave, who sink to rest,
By all their country's wishes blessed!
When Spring, with dewy fingers cold,
Returns to deck their hallowed mould,
She there shall dress a sweeter sod
Than Fancy's feet have ever trod.
 May they rest in peace,
 In peace for ever rest!

2 By fairy hands their knell is rung;
By forms unseen their dirge is sung;
There Honor comes, a pilgrim gray,
To bless the turf that wraps their clay;

And Freedom shall awhile repair,
To dwell a weeping hermit there!
May they rest in peace,
In peace for ever rest!

145. *" There is a calm for those who weep."*   8s & 4s.

1 There is a calm for those who weep,
    A rest for weary pilgrims found;
They softly lie, and sweetly sleep,
    Low in the ground.

2 The storm that racks the wintry sky
    No more disturbs their deep repose
Than summer evening's latest sigh,
    That shuts the rose.

3 I long to lay this painful head
    And aching heart beneath the soil;
To slumber, in that dreamless bed,
    From all my toil.

4 The soul, of origin divine,
    God's glorious image, freed from clay,
In heaven's eternal sphere shall shine,
    A star of day.

5 The sun is but a spark of fire,
    A transient meteor in the sky;
The soul, immortal as its Sire,
    Shall never die.

146. *" Thou art to pass over Jordan this day."*   8s & 7s.

1 My days are gliding swiftly by,
    And I, a pilgrim stranger,
Would not detain them as they fly,—
    Those hours of toil and danger:

For now we stand on Jordan's strand,
    Our friends are passing over,
And, just before, the shining shore
    We may almost discover.

2 Our absent King the watchword gave,—
    "Let every lamp be burning;"
We look afar across the wave,
    Our distant home discerning:
        For now we stand, &c.

3 Should coming days be dark and cold,
    We will not yield to sorrow;
For hope will sing with courage bold,
    "There's glory on the morrow:"
        For now we stand, &c.

4 Let storms of woe in whirlwinds rise,
    Each cord on earth to sever,—
There, bright and joyous in the skies—
    There is our home for ever:
        For now we stand, &c.

147.   *"Dust to dust."*   C. M.

1 CALM on the bosom of thy God,
    Young spirit, rest thee now!
Even while with us thy footsteps trod,
    His seal was on thy brow.

2 Dust, to its narrow house beneath!
    Soul, to its place on high!
They that have seen thy look in death,
    No more may fear to die.

3 Lone are the paths, and sad the bowers,
    Whence thy meek smile is gone;
But, oh! a brighter home than ours,
    In heaven, is now thine own.

148. *Nunc dimittis.* 7s.

1 'Tis enough—the hour is come;
Now within the silent tomb
Let this mortal frame decay,
Mingled with its kindred clay.

2 Since thy mercies, oft of old
By thy chosen seers foretold,
Faithful now and steadfast prove,
God of truth, and God of love.

3 Since at length, my aged eye
Sees the day-spring from on high;
Sun of righteousness, to thee,
Lo! the nations bow the knee.

4 And the realms of distant kings
Own the healing of thy wings.
Those whom death had overspread
With his dark and dreary shade,

5 Lift their eyes, and from afar
Hail the light of Jacob's star,
Waiting till the promised ray
Turn their darkness into day.

6 See the beam intensely shed,
Shine o'er Zion's favored head;
Never may they hence remove,
God of truth, and God of love.

149. *" We will not deplore thee."* 12s.

1 Thou art gone to the grave! but we will not deplore thee,
    Though sorrows and darkness encompass the tomb;
The Saviour hath passed through its portals before thee,
    And the lamp of his love is thy guide through the gloom.

2 Thou art gone to the grave! we no longer behold thee,
  Nor tread the rough paths of the world by thy side;
But the wide arms of mercy are spread to enfold thee,
  And sinners may hope, for the Sinless hath died.

3 Thou art gone to the grave! and, its mansion forsaking,
  Perchance thy weak spirit in doubt lingered long:
But the sunshine of glory beamed bright on thy waking,
  And full on thine ear burst the seraphim's song.

4 Thou art gone to the grave! but we will not deplore thee,
  Since God was thy Ransom, thy Guardian, and Guide:
He gave thee, he took thee, and he will restore thee;
  And death has no sting, for the Saviour hath died.

150. *Eternity.* L. M.

1 Eternity—eternity!
  O bright, O blest eternity!
  Which Jesus hath obtained for those
  Who seek in him their sure repose;
  A little while they suffer here,
  But lo! eternity is near:
  Eternity—eternity!

2 Eternity—eternity!
  Soon shall these eyes thy wonders see;
  Oh, may I now the world despise,
  And upward raise my thankful eyes,
  And seek the joys that shall abide,
  From sin and sorrow purified:
  O bright, O blest eternity!

3 Eternity—eternity!
  Prepare me for eternity;
  Now grant me, Lord, thy humble mind,
  To all my Father's will resigned:

Now give me faith that rests on thee;
Lord! in thy love, remember me,
In time and in eternity.

151. *"Are they not all ministering spirits?"* P. M.

1 How cheering the thought, that the spirits in bliss
Will bow their bright wings to a world such as this;
Will leave the sweet joys of the mansions above,
To breathe o'er our bosoms some message of love.

2 They come, on the wings of the morning they come,
Impatient to lead some poor wanderer home,
Some pilgrim to snatch from this stormy abode,
And lay him to rest in the arms of his God.

MISCELLANEOUS.

152. *The Seasons.* 7s & 6s.

1 When Spring unlocks the flowers,
To paint the laughing soil;
When Summer's balmy showers
Refresh the mower's toil;
When winter binds in frosty chains
The fallow and the flood,
In God the earth rejoiceth still,
And owns his Maker good.

2 The birds that wake the morning,
And those that love the shade;
The winds that sweep the mountain,
Or lull the drowsy glade;
The sun that from his amber bower,
Rejoiceth in his way,

The moon and stars their Maker's name
  In silent pomp display.

3 Shall man, the lord of nature,
  Expectant of the sky,
Shall man alone unthankful,
  His little praise deny?
No, let the year forsake his course,
  The seasons cease to be,
Thee, Father, must we always love,
  Creator, honor thee.

4 The flowers of spring may wither,
  The hope of summer fade,
The autumn droop in winter,
  The birds forsake the shade,
The winds be lulled, the sun and moon
  Forget their old decree,
But we, in nature's latest hour,
  O Lord, will cling to thee.

153. *Miriam's Song.*

1 Sound the loud timbrel, o'er Egypt's dark sea—
Jehovah has triumphed, his people are free.
Sing, for the pride of the tyrant is broken,
  His chariot, his horsemen, all splendid and brave,
How vain was their boasting, the Lord hath but spoken,
  And chariots and horsemen are sunk in the wave!
Sound the loud timbrel, o'er Egypt's dark sea,
Jehovah has triumphed, his people are free.

2 Praise for the victory, praise to the Lord,
His word was our arrow, his breath was our sword!
Who shall return to tell Egypt the story,
  Of those she sent forth in the hour of her pride?
The Lord hath looked out from his pillar of glory,
  And all her brave thousands are dashed in the tide.
Sound the loud timbrel, o'er Egypt's dark sea,
Jehovah has triumphed, his people are free.

154. *"Save thy people, and bless thine inheritance."* 8s & 6s.

1 From foes that would the land devour;
From guilty pride, and lust of power;
From wild sedition's lawless hour;
　From yoke of slavery;
From blinded zeal, by faction led;
From giddy change, by fancy bred;
From poisoned error's serpent head,
　Good Lord, preserve us free!

2 Defend, O God, with guardian hand,
The laws and rulers of our land,
And grant thy churches grace to stand
　In faith and unity!
Thy Spirit's help of thee we crave,
That thy Messiah, sent to save,
Returning to the world, might have
　A people serving thee!

155. *"So didst thou lead thy people."* L. M.

1 O God, beneath thy guiding hand,
　Our exiled fathers crossed the sea;
And when they trod the wintery strand,
　With prayer and psalm they worshipped thee.

2 Thou heard'st, well pleased, the song, the prayer:
　Thy blessing came; and still its power
Shall onward through all ages bear
　The memory of that holy hour.

3 Laws, freedom, truth, and faith in God
　Came with those exiles o'er the waves;
And where their pilgrim feet have trod,
　The God they trusted guards their graves.

4 And here thy name, O God of love,
  Their children's children shall adore,
 Till these eternal hills remove,
  And spring adorns the earth no more.

156.   *"God save the State!"*   6s & 4s.

1 God bless our native land!
 Firm may she ever stand,
  Through storm and night;
 When the wild tempests rave,
 Ruler of winds and wave,
 Do thou our country save
  By thy great might.

2 For her our prayer shall rise
 To God, above the skies;
  On him we wait:
 Thou who art ever nigh,
 Guarding with watchful eye,
 To thee aloud we cry,
  God save the State!

157.   *God and our Country.*

1 Flag of the heroes who left us their glory,
  Borne through their battle-fields' thunder and flame,
 Blazoned in song and illumined in story,
  Wave o'er us all who inherit their fame!
    Up with our banner bright,
    Sprinkled with starry light;
  Spread its fair emblems from mountain to shore;
    While, through the sounding sky,
    Loud rings the Nation's cry—
  Union and Liberty! one evermore!

2 Lord of the Universe! shield us and guide us,
  Trusting thee always, through shadow and sun.
 Thou hast united us; who shall divide us?
  Keep us, oh! keep us, the many in one.
    Up with our banner bright, &c.

158. *My Country, 'tis of thee.* 6s & 4s.

1 My country, 'tis of thee,
  Sweet land of liberty,
    Of thee I sing;
  Land where my fathers died,
  Land of the Pilgrims' pride,
  From every mountain's side
    Let freedom ring.

2 My native country! thee,
  Land of the noble free,
    Thy name I love;
  I love thy rocks and rills;
  Thy woods and templed hills,
  My heart with rapture thrills,
    Like that above.

3 Let music swell the breeze,
  And ring from all the trees,
    Sweet freedom's song;
  Let mortal tongues awake,
  Let all that breathe partake;
  Let rocks their silence break,
    The sound prolong.

4 Our fathers' God! to thee
  Author of liberty!
    To thee we sing;
  Long may our land be bright
  With freedom's holy light;
  Protect us by thy might,
    Great God our King!

159.   *The Progress of Freedom.*   P. M

1 Oppression shall not always reign;
    There comes a brighter day,
When freedom, burst from every chain,
    Shall have triumphant way.
Then right shall over might prevail,
And truth, like hero armed in mail,
The hosts of tyrant wrong assail,
    And hold eternal sway.

2 What voice shall bid the progress stay
    Of truth's victorious car?
What arm arrest the growing day,
    Or quench the solar star?
What reckless soul, though stout and strong,
Shall dare bring back the ancient wrong,
Oppression's guilty night prolong,
    And freedom's morning bar?

3 The hour of triumph comes apace,
    The fated, promised hour,
When earth upon a ransomed race
    Her bounteous gifts shall shower.
Ring, Liberty, thy glorious bell!
Bid high thy sacred banner swell!
Let trump on trump the triumph tell
    Of Heaven's redeeming power.

Doxology.   L. M.

Immortal praise to God be given,
By all in earth and all in heaven;
The First, the Last, who reigns alone,
And fills an undivided throne.

Doxology.   C. M.

1 Thou art the First, and thou the Last,
    Time centres all in thee,
The Almighty God who was and is,
    And evermore shall be.

2 To thee let every tongue be praise,
    And every heart be love,
All grateful honors paid on earth,
    And nobler songs above.

APPENDIX.

THE Venite, &c., which follow, with the corresponding versified Hymns, are appended for the convenience of any Churches who are accustomed, or may please, to use Chanting at Morning Service.

Each Chant is designed to be closed with this Doxology:

NOW unto the King eternal, immortal, invisible, the only wise God;
Be honor and glory, through Jesus Christ, for ever and ever. Amen.

Or the Gloria Patri, thus:

GLORY be to the Father, Almighty God, through Jesus Christ our Lord;
As it was in the beginning, is now, and ever shall be, world without end. *Amen.*

I.

Venite, exultemus Domino.

O COME, let us sing unto the Lord; let us heartily rejoice in the strength of our salvation.
Let us come before his presence with thanksgiving; and show ourselves glad in him with psalms.
For the Lord is a great God; and a great King above all gods.

In his hand are all the corners of the earth; and the strength of the hills is his also.

The sea is his, and he made it; and his hands prepared the dry land.

O come, let us worship and fall down, and kneel before the Lord our Maker.

For he is the Lord our God; and we are the people of his pasture, and the sheep of his hand.

O worship the Lord in the beauty of holiness; let the whole earth stand in awe of him.

For he cometh, for he cometh to judge the earth; and with righteousness to judge the world, and the people with his truth.

Or this Hymn:

PUBLIC WORSHIP. L. M.

O COME, loud anthems let us sing,
   Loud thanks to our Almighty King;
For we our voices high should raise,
When our salvation's rock we praise.

Into his presence let us haste,
To thank him for his favors past;
To him address, in joyful songs,
The praise that to his Name belongs.

The depths of earth are in his hand,
Her secret wealth at his command;
The strength of hills, that threat the skies,
Subjected to his empire lies.

The rolling ocean's vast abyss
By the same sovereign right is his;

'Tis moved by his almighty hand,
That formed and fixed the solid land.

O let us to his courts repair,
And bow with adoration there;
Down on our knees devoutly all
Before the Lord our Maker fall.

II.

Jubilate Deo.

O BE joyful in the Lord, all ye lands: serve the Lord with gladness, and come before his presence with a song.

Be ye sure that the Lord he is God; it is he that hath made us, and not we ourselves; we are his people, and the sheep of his pasture.

O go your way into his gates with thanksgiving, and into his courts with praise; be thankful unto him, and speak good of his Name.

For the Lord is gracious, his mercy is everlasting; and his truth endureth from generation to generation.

Or this Hymn:

SACRED JOY.   11s & 8s.

BE joyful in God, all ye lands of the earth,
  O serve him with gladness and fear;
Exult in his presence with music and mirth,
  With love and devotion draw near.

Jehovah is God, and Jehovah alone,
  Creator and Ruler o'er all;
And we are his people—his sceptre we own;
  His sheep, and we follow his call.

Oh! enter his gates with thanksgiving and song,
  Your vows in his temple proclaim;
His praise in melodious accordance prolong,
  And bless his adorable Name.

For good is the Lord, inexpressibly good,
  And we are the work of his hand;
His mercy and truth from eternity stood,
  And shall to eternity stand.

III.

Miserere mei, Deus.

BE merciful unto me, O God, be merciful unto me, for my soul trusteth in thee.

Be thou exalted, O God, above the heavens, and let thy glory be above all the earth.

My heart is fixed, O God, my heart is fixed; I will sing, and give praise.

Awake up, my glory; awake, lute and harp; I myself will awake right early.

I will give thanks unto thee, O Lord, among the people, and I will sing unto thee among the nations.

For the greatness of thy mercy reacheth unto the heavens, and thy truth unto the clouds.

Be thou exalted, O God, above the heavens, and let thy glory be above all the earth.

Or this Hymn:

PRAISE FOR PROTECTION.   L. M.

MY God, in whom are all the springs
  Of boundless love and grace unknown;
Hide me beneath thy spreading wings,
  Till the dark cloud is overblown.

Up to the heavens I send my cry;
The Lord will my desires perform;
He sends his angels from the sky,
And saves me from the threatening storm.

My heart is fixed; my song shall raise
Immortal honors to thy Name;
Awake, my tongue, to sound his praise,
My tongue, the glory of my frame.

High o'er the earth his mercy reigns,
And reaches to the utmost sky;
His truth to endless years remains,
When lower worlds dissolve and die.

Be thou exalted, O my God,
Above the heavens, where angels dwell;
Thy power on earth be known abroad,
And land to land thy wonders tell.

IV.

Benedictus.

BLESSED be the Lord God of Israel; for he hath visited and redeemed his people;

And hath raised up a mighty salvation for us, in the house of his servant David;

As he spake by the mouth of his holy Prophets, which have been since the world began;

That we should be saved from our enemies, and from the hand of all that hate us.

To perform the mercy promised to our forefathers, and to remember his holy covenant;

To perform the oath which he sware to our forefather Abraham, that he would give us;

That we being delivered out of the hand of our enemies, might serve him without fear;

In holiness and righteousness before him all the days of our life.

Or this Hymn:

MERCY OF GOD. S. M.

RAISE your triumphal songs
   To an immortal tune;
Let all the earth resound the deeds
   Celestial grace has done:

Sing how eternal love
   Its chief Beloved chose,
And bade him raise our wretched race
   From their abyss of woes.

Now, sinners, dry your tears;
   Let hopeless sorrow cease;
Bow to the sceptre of His love,
   And take the offered peace.

Lord, we obey thy call;
   We lay an humble claim
To the salvation Thou hast brought,
   And love and praise thy Name.

V.

Lætatus sum.

I WAS glad when they said unto me, We will go into the house of the Lord.

Our feet shall stand in thy gates, O Jerusalem.

O pray for the peace of Jerusalem; they shall prosper that love thee.

Peace be within thy walls, and plenteousness within thy palaces.

For my brethren and companions' sake, I will wish thee prosperity.

Yea, because of the house of the Lord our God, I will seek to do thee good.

Or this Hymn:

THE CITY OF GOD. 8s & 7s.

BLESSED city, heavenly Salem,
    Vision dear, whence peace doth spring;
Brighter than the heart can fancy,
    Mansion of the highest King;
O how glorious are the praises
    Which of thee the prophets sing!

To this temple, where we call thee,
    Come, O Lord of Hosts, to-day!
With thy wonted loving-kindness,
    Hear thy people as they pray;
And thy fullest benediction
    Shed within its walls for aye.

Here vouchsafe to all thy servants
    That they supplicate to gain;
Here to have and hold for ever
    Those good things their pray'rs obtain;
And hereafter in thy glory
    With thy blessed ones to reign.

The Gloria in Excelsis and Te Deum will be found when desired for Morning use, at pp. 24 and 28 respectively, of the Vespers.

TABLE OF FIRST LINES.

		PAGE
Again, as evening's shadow falls	*Prudentius—Longfellow's Vespers.*	9
A holy air is breathing round	*Longfellow's Coll.*	66
All hail, the power of Jesus' name!	*Duncan.*	58
Angel, roll the stone away	*J. Scott.*	61
As the harp-strings only render	*Adam St. Victor.*	73
At midnight bursts the cry	*Ambrosian Hymn.*	74
At the cross her station keeping	*Stabat Mater—Caswall.*	44
Awake, thou wintry earth	*Thos. Blackburn.*	56
Awake, ye saints, awake	*Cotterill.*	3
Behold the western evening light!	*W. B. O. Peabody.*	11
Be near us, O Father! through night's silent hour	*Breviary.*	7
Breast the wave, Christian, when it is strongest	*Staughton.*	86
Brightest and best of the sons of the morning	*Heber.*	40
Calm me, my God, and keep me calm	*Bonar.*	85
Calm on the bosom of thy God	*Hemans.*	95
Children of God lack nothing	*Newton.*	27
Come, Holy Ghost, our hearts inspire	*Wesley.*	47
Come, let our voices join	*Pratt's Coll.*	90
Come, thou Fount of every blessing	*Robinson.*	84
Come to the ark, come to the ark	*Beard's Coll.*	78
Daughter of Zion, awake from thy sadness!	*Fitzgerald's Coll.*	50
Depart awhile, each thought of care	*Lyra Catholica.*	12
Do I delight in sorrow's dress	*Morrison.*	88
Eternity—Eternity!	*Wülffer.*	97
Fading, still fading, the last beam is shining	*Longfellow's Coll.*	5
Father, I know that all my life	*Anna L. Waring.*	23
Father supreme! thou high and holy One	*Longfellow's Coll.*	6
Father, we look up to thee	*Wesleyan.*	31
Flag of the heroes who left us their glory	*O. W. Holmes.*	101
For all thy saints, O God	*Ancient Hymns.*	87
From foes that would the land devour	*Heber.*	100
From God, thou Holy Ghost	*Montgomery.*	48
Gently, Lord! oh, gently lead us	*Hastings.*	26
Glorious God, we come to bless thee		17
God bless our native land	*J. S. Dwight.*	101

TABLE OF FIRST LINES.

		PAGE
God is love; his mercy brightens	Bowring.	25
God is my strong salvation	Montgomery.	26
God named Love, whose fount thou art	Mrs. Browning.	71
Great Author of my being	Wesley.	82
Great God! the followers of thy Son	H. Ware, Jr.	30
Guide me, O thou great Jehovah	Oliver.	35
Hail to the Lord's Anointed	Montgomery.	41
Hallelujah! raise, oh, raise	Conder.	23
Hark! the herald angels sing	Episcopal Coll.	51
Hark! the song of Jubilee!	Montgomery.	68
Hark! the vesper hymn is stealing		4
Hark! through the courts of heaven	Sabbath Hymn Book.	81
Hath not thy heart within thee burned	Bulfinch.	42
Hear, Father, hear our prayer!	Longfellow's Coll.	88
Hear us, heavenly Father, hear us!	Longfellow's Vespers.	9
Heralds of creation! cry	Montgomery.	39
Here in the broken bread	Furness.	56
Her eyes are homes of silent prayer	A. Tennyson.	81
Holiest! breathe an evening blessing	Edmeston.	8
Holy Ghost, the Infinite!	Sabbath Hymn Book.	49
Holy Ghost! with light divine	Reed.	46
Holy Spirit, Lord of light	From King Robert—Caswall.	47
Holy Spirit; Love Divine	Sabbath Hymn Book.	63
How cheering the thought, that the spirits in bliss	Cunningham.	93
How sleep the brave, who sink to rest	Collins.	93
I love my God, but with no love of mine	Mad. Guyon.	79
In heavenly love abiding	Sabbath Hymn Book.	83
In the cross of Christ we glory	Bowring.	60
Is there a lone and dreary hour	Mrs. Gilman.	73
It came upon the midnight clear	E. H. Sears.	42
Jesus, lover of my soul	C. Wesley.	43
Jesus, the strength of angels strong	St. Bernard.	71
Jesus, the very thought of thee	St. Bernard.	44
Jews were wrought to cruel madness	W. J. Fox.	87
Lift up your hearts! Yes, I will lift	Lyra Catholica.	36
Lift your glad voices in triumph on high	H. Ware, Jr.	61
Light of life, seraphic fire!	C. Wesley.	29
Lord, have mercy when we pray	Milman.	32
Lord of all being throned afar	O. W. Holmes.	22
Lord of eternal purity!	Caswall.	20
Lord, with fervor I would praise thee	Episcopal Coll.	84
Lord, who ordainest for mankind	Original here—W. C. Bryant.	89
Lowly and solemn be	Mrs. Hemans.	75
Meek and lowly, pure and holy		77
Mighty One, before whose face	W. C. Bryant.	68
My country, 'tis of thee	S. F. Smith.	102
My days are gliding swiftly by	Sabbath Hymn Book.	94
My soul doth long for thee	Brydges.	77

TABLE OF FIRST LINES.

		PAGE
Nearer, my God, to thee	*S. F. Adams.*	10
No war or battle's sound	*Dr. Gardiner from Milton.*	50
Now that the sun is beaming bright	*Ambrose.*	1
Now, when the dusky shades of night retreating	*Ancient.*	1
O Almighty God of love	*Wesleyan.*	27
O blest Creator of the light	*Ambrosian—Longfellow's Vespers.*	10
O bread to pilgrims given	*Thos. Aquinas.*	65
O God, beneath thy guiding hand	*L. Bacon.*	100
O God, my heart is fixed, 'tis bent	*Cudworth.*	57
O God, whose dread and dazzling brow	*W. C. Bryant.*	36
Oh for a heart to praise my God!	*Wesleyan.*	86
Oh, happy day, that fixed my choice	*Doddridge.*	80
Oh, what though our feet may not tread where Christ trod	*Whittier.*	53
Oh, worship the King all glorious above	*Grant.*	24
O Love Divine, that stooped to share	*O. W. Holmes.*	18
Open, Lord, mine inward ear	*Methodist Coll.*	32
Oppression shall not always reign	*H. Ware, Jr.*	103
O, richly, Father, have I been	*W. H. Furness.*	28
O sacred Head, now wounded!	*Paul Gerhard.*	55
O thou great Friend to all the sons of men	*Theodore Parker.*	53
O thou pure Light of souls that love	*Ambrosian.*	15
O Thou to whom, in ancient time	*J. Pierpont.*	33
O Thou whose power stupendous	*Italian.*	29
Out of the depths of woe	*Montgomery.*	76
Peace, troubled soul, whose plaintive moan		75
People of the living God	*Montgomery.*	67
Planted in Christ, the living Vine	*S. F. Smith.*	66
Ride on, ride on in majesty!	*Milman.*	54
Rocked in the cradle of the deep	*Mrs. Willard.*	14
Rock of Ages! cleft for me	*Toplady.*	53
Saviour, who thy flock art feeding	*Episcopal Coll.*	64
See, daylight is fading o'er earth and o'er ocean	*Heber.*	14
Shout the glad tidings, exultingly sing	*Episcopal Coll.*	58
Sister, thou wast mild and lovely	*S. F. Smith.*	93
Slowly, by God's hand unfurled	*Furness.*	8
Smile praises, O sky	*Mediæval Hymn.*	19
Sound the loud timbrel, o'er Egypt's dark sea	*Thos. Moore.*	99
Sovereign and transforming grace	*F. H. Hedge.*	69
Spirit divine! attend our prayer	*Reed.*	45
Strike the cymbal, roll the timbrel	*Rohr's Coll.*	59
Sweet is the light of Sabbath eve	*Edmeston.*	5
Tarry with me, O my Saviour!	*Sabbath Hymn Book.*	92
The Apostles on the mountain stand	*Venerable Bede.*	62
The day expires!	*Freylinghausen.*	15
Thee in the hymns of morn we praise	*Breviary.*	15
Thee we adore, eternal Lord!	*Ancient.*	24
The mellow eve is gliding	*Sacred Songs.*	13
The night is come, wherein at last we rest	*Bohemian Brethren.*	18

TABLE OF FIRST LINES.

		PAGE
The praying spirit breathe	*Methodist Coll.*	34
There is a calm for those who weep	*Montgomery.*	94
The spirits of the loved and the departed	*Longfellow's Coll.*	7
The sun is set. I mark the stars as gleaming, one by one	*Bishop Mant.*	21
They who seek the throne of grace	*Hymns of the Ages.*	30
Thou art gone to the grave! but we will not deplore thee	*Heber.*	56
Thou art, O God, the life and light	*Thos. Moore.*	38
Thou Brightness of the Father's ray	*From Ambrose, by Neale.*	
Though faint, yet pursuing, we go on our way	*Sabbath Hymn Book.*	79
Thou whose almighty word	*Marriott.*	70
Through the love of God our Saviour	*Sabbath Hymn Book.*	83
'Tis enough, the hour is come	*Merrick.*	96
'Tis Nature's time for prayer	*Hymns of the Ages.*	16
To Him who children blest	*Disciples' H. Book.*	64
To thee, O God in heaven	*Disciples' H. Book.*	64
To thine eternal arms, O God	*T. W. Higginson.*	72
Up! up! the day is breaking	*Paul Gerhard.*	73
When first the Spirit of our God	*Keble.*	63
When I am weak, I'm strong	*N. L. Frothingham.*	72
When marshalled on the nightly plain	*H. K. White.*	52
When shall the voice of singing	*Pratt's Coll.*	89
When Spring unlocks the flowers	*Heber.*	98
When, streaming from the eastern skies	*Sir R. Grant.*	3
When the sun gloriously comes forth from the ocean		4
While thou, O my God, art my help and defender	*W. Young.*	37
While we here remember thee	*J. Pierpont.*	67
Who hath a right like us to sing	*Wesley.*	91
With silence only as their benediction	*J. G. Whittier.*	33

www.ingramcontent.com/pod-product-compliance
Lightning Source LLC
Chambersburg PA
CBHW020808230426
43666CB00007B/913